T0146741

The Feast Days of the Lord
In Light of the New Testament

MICHAEL A. LESLIE

WESTBOW
PRESS®
A DIVISION OF THOMAS NELSON
& ZONDERVAN

WestBow Press books may be ordered through booksellers or by contacting:

WestBow Press
A Division of Thomas Nelson & Zondervan
1663 Liberty Drive
Bloomington, IN 47403
www.westbowpress.com
1 (866) 928-1240

Interior Artwork Credit: KC Moore

Scripture taken from the King James Version of the Bible.

ISBN: 978-1-5127-9336-9 (sc)
ISBN: 978-1-5127-9338-3 (hc)
ISBN: 978-1-5127-9337-6 (e)

Library of Congress Control Number: 2017909982

Print information available on the last page.

WestBow Press rev. date: 7/6/2017

*To my wonderful, loving wife Nancy, who has stood
by my side in encouragement and loyal support*

Contents

Preface

This work on the feast days of the Lord had its roots many years ago as I became a Christian and began to search the scriptures. For many years, I have enjoyed gold mining, but long before I went gold mining, the preface of the book *How to Enjoy the Bible* by E. W. Bullinger inspired me. He describes a married couple who had a deep desire to study and know God's Word. I also had this deep desire. I loved sifting through God's Word, looking for His hidden gems and nuggets He had for me.

As I continued my journey, I wrote many essays and teachings that were never intended to be published. As my research continued, I found myself asking God questions as I read His Word, inquiries I wanted answered so His Word was more real to me. I would read a section in His Word and ask such questions as, "What does this mean? When in time did this happen? What was going on in the culture at the setting of this scripture?" I have been taught that God's Word reveals itself in numerous ways. Some call it "biblical research principles," but I would refer to it as recognizing His patterns and design.

The Hebrew word *tabnit* means to "build, plan, or design a structure." I understood these words from being a general contractor for over thirty years. In understanding how God set things up (e.g., His reckoning of time or His meaning of words), the whole Bible began to open up for me. I learned from E. W. Bullinger a biblical term regarding scripture as having "scope." Scope comes with time in studying the Bible, taking small pieces of the puzzle, putting them together, and then stepping back to see the larger picture. My heart's desire is to understand God's Word as a whole, and I continue to keep digging and searching His Word for the gems He has in store for me.

Acknowledgements

I owe my style of research and teaching to two men who influenced me early on in my Christian leadership development: Reverend David Bergey and Reverend Doug Seed. I spent a number of years working closely with them in service and teaching Bible fellowships, including participating in a yearlong project in 1982 searching the Bible and documenting alternative scriptures for the "Power for Abundant Living Class" taught by Dr. Victor Paul Wierwille in 1953.

I also owe much thanks to some more recent individuals such as Reverend Jan Magiera, who accomplished extensive work translating the New Testament from the Peshitta text of Aramaic. She has opened my eyes to realize more deeply that God wants His Word known to all men and that He can inspire anyone to do so.

I am grateful to have met a young man, whose father I knew. This young rising musician Aaron Schaffer, wrote a song that ranked number one in the Christian music chart. He explained to me how God inspired him to write the song. His story inspired me to continue in this endeavor.

Our special thanks to Don and Debra Hendrickson, who gave us their loving critique. I would also like to thank my loyal friends and companions, Reverend Tom Smith and Reverend Ken Petty, who have loved me up on this journey.

Lastly, words could not describe out thanks to KC Moore, an award winning California artist, for her heart, commitment, and inspiration in providing the artwork for this project.

Introduction

The writers of the New Testament used their backgrounds, languages, and the culture surrounding them in their writings. From the book of Acts through the book of Revelation, there are five primary writers: Luke, Paul, Peter, James, and John. All except Luke had a Hebrew upbringing, and he would have drawn off his Hebrew background and experiences in his writings of the Epistles. An understanding of the Old Testament culture, practices, and ways is crucial to more fully appreciate many sections of the New Testament.

In this book, the reader will gain a greater knowledge of God's timetable and the understanding of the Hebrew culture specifically in light of God's feasts, their calendars and reckoning of time, prophecies that have been fulfilled, as well as other prophecies still hanging in the balance. Whole sections of the Gospels and church epistles will come to light with an understanding of what these feasts were all about and their parallels to what Christ accomplished for us.

Hebrews 10:1 says, "For the law having a shadow of good things to come, and not the very image of the things, can never with those sacrifices which they offered year by year continually make the comers thereunto perfect."

These "good things" were the good news of Jesus Christ. The law, which included the feast days, was a shadow of things to come in the future. The feast days were a foreshadowing of the coming Messiah.

Romans 15:4 reads, "For whatsoever things were written aforetime were written for our learning, that we through patience and comfort of the scriptures might have hope."

The Old Testament was for our learning and so we might have hope. The feast days were to be a celebration. Most included an aspect of rejoicing and partaking with food. It was a time of communion with God and one another in recognition that God was their provider, "I am the Lord your God."

May God grant you a greater understanding of His feasts through this book and the unveiling of His Word.

Chapter 1
God's Reckoning of Time

What is the date today? When did today begin? When did this week begin? When does next month begin? When does next year begin? Here in Western civilization, we have accepted definitions for these questions that have stood for many centuries. It is hard for us to think in any other way about how time was reckoned. However, if we are to understand timekeeping from a biblical perspective, we need to understand God's way of reckoning time.

A Day

To begin with, what is a day? In recent times, we determine a day to be that period of time between one midnight and the next. On the other hand, according to the Bible, a day begins at sundown, extends through the darkness of night and the sunlit period that follows, and ends with the next sundown.

In Genesis, God defines what a day is. "And God said, Let there be light: and there was light. And God saw the light, that it was good: and God divided the light from the darkness. And God called the light Day, and the darkness he called Night. And the evening and the morning were the first day" (Gen. 1:3–5).

Notice "evening and morning." Note that evening comes first. For many cultures, evening marks the start of a new day. Western culture starts a new day at midnight. "Evening and morning" is a figure of speech called "synecdoche," meaning the parts are representative of the whole. God defines "day" two ways in these verses. Day or daylight refers to the time between sunrise and sunset. "Evening and morning" refers to a day as a twenty-four hour period.

Hours of the Day

Daylight period was divided into twelve hours; evening period was divided into twelve hours. "Jesus answered, Are there not twelve hours in the day? If any man walk in the day, he stumbleth not, because he seeth the light of this world. But if a man walk in the night, he stumbleth, because there is no light in him" (John 11:9–10).

In the gospel times, a period of the day was divided into four watches. "Watch ye therefore: for ye know not when the master of the house cometh, at *even* [evening], or at *midnight*, or at the *cockcrowing*, or in the *morning*" (Mark 13:35; emphasis added).

Here four watches are referenced. Each comprised a three-hour period. In Hebrew culture, a reckoning of the hour may refer to what hour it was after sunset or after sunrise. For example, the third hour of the day would be 9:00 a.m., if sunrise were 6:00 a.m.

A Week

What is a week? The week begins when Sunday begins, and it ends when the next Saturday ends. In other words, a week is simply a seven-day cycle. Every seven days, a new week begins. Bearing in mind that days have a different beginning and ending time of reckoning time, weeks are otherwise the same in Bible times. "And on the seventh day God ended his work which he had made; and he rested on the seventh day from all his work which he had made" (Gen. 2:2)

To ensure that this practice would not be lost, it was legislated for the children of Israel by God through Moses. Consider again the commandment,

> Remember the sabbath day, to keep it holy. Six days you shall labor, and do all thy work: But the seventh day is the sabbath of the Lord thy God: in it thou shalt not do any work ... For in six days the Lord God made heaven

and earth, the sea, and all that in them is, and rested the seventh day: wherefore the Lord blessed the sabbath day, and hallowed it (Ex. 20:8–11).

In the Bible, the word "week" is the Hebrew word *shavua*, which is from the word *sheva* and means "seven." Since everyone in the world has been keeping time in this way from the beginning, there is extremely little chance that the seven-day cycle has ever been disrupted or lost. The Hebrews named their days of the week by counting toward the Sabbath. For example, Sunday was the first day before the Sabbath. The sixth day of the week was also called "the day of preparation." (See Josephus, Ant.16.163.)

A Week in the Hebrew Calendar			
Hebrew	**Transliteration**	**Hebrew Meaning**	**English Name**
יום ראשון	Yom Rishon	First Day	Sunday
יום שני	Yom Sheni	Second Day	Monday
יום שלישי	Yom Shlishi	Third Day	Tuesday
יום רבעי	Yom R'vi'i	Fourth Day	Wednesday
יום חמישי	Yom Chamishi	Fifth Day	Thursday
יום ששי	Yom Shishi	Sixth Day	Friday
יום שבת	Yom Shabbat	Sabbath Day	Saturday

A Month

How are months reckoned? Our Gregorian calendar divides the 365 days of the year into twelve months of varying lengths. Because a solar year actually has roughly 365.25 days, we need to add an extra day every four years to the month of February. Otherwise, after many years, those quarter days would add up to a significant period of time and throw the calendar out of synchronization with the solar year. Because the solar year is more accurately 365.242199 days, on rare occasions we need to tweak the calendar a little. But the Gregorian calendar works well enough that we keep using it. So months in our calendar are simply handy divisions of the solar year.

According to the Bible, a month is reckoned from the first appearance of a new moon to the next appearance of a new moon. The Hebrew word for month is *chodesh*, which literally means "new moon." Psalm 104:19 says, "He appointed the moon for seasons: the sun knoweth his going down." This word "seasons" is the word *chodesh*.

It is easy to determine when a new month begins with this way of reckoning the month. You simply go outside in the evening and look. When you see the first little sliver of a new moon, you start counting the days of the next month. You keep counting days until the moon goes through its phases. When you see the next new moon, you stop counting in the old month and start counting a new month. It takes approximately 29.5 days, or 29.530587 days to be more exact, from new moon to new moon.

Of course, these months had different names. Here are the names given to these months according to the Jewish calendar and when they begin corresponding to the Gregorian calendar:

Months of the Hebrew Calendar				
Number	Hebrew	Transliteration	Length	Modern Calendar
1	ניסן	Nisan	30 days	March-April
2	אייר	Iyar	29 days	April-May
3	סיון	Sivan	30 days	May-June
4	מוז	Tammuz	29 days	June-July
5	אב	Av	30 days	July-August
6	לול	Elul	29 days	August-September
7	תשרי	Tishri	30 days	September-October
8	חשון	Cheshvan	29 or 30 days	October-November
9	כסל	Chislev	30 or 29 days	November-December
10	טבת	Tevet	29 days	December-January
11	שבט	Shevat	30 days	January-February
12	אדר	Adar	30 days	February-March
13	ואדר	Adar II (in leap years)	29 days	February-March

A Year

The Hebrews used two calendars. One was the civil calendar, which began with our months September and October. It was the only calendar in use until God gave Moses a holy calendar on Mount Sinai (the sacred calendar). The oldest Hebrew calendar was the Gezer calendar found at Tel Gezer, Palestine, around 925 BC.

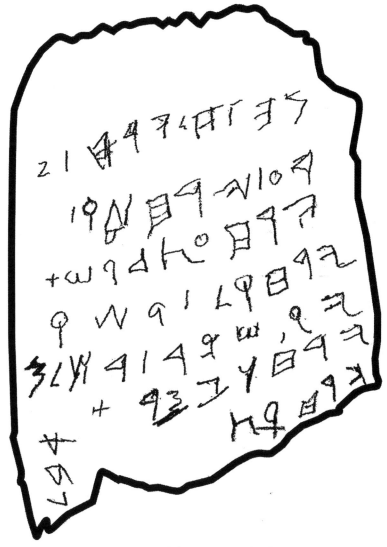

Drawing of the Gezer Calendar.

In Hebrew folklore, it was believed that God created the heavens and earth in the seventh month called Tishri. It has been widely believed that Jesus Christ was born on Tishri 1. It is also believed that Adam and Noah were born in the month, Tishri.

The civil calendar was used for dating the reign of kings and the anointing of a king on Tishri 1. Understanding the use of two different calendars helps clear up many discrepancies in the Bible.

Let us now see how God instituted the holy or sacred calendar. "And the LORD spake unto Moses and Aaron in the land of Egypt saying, This month shall be unto you the beginning of months: it shall be the first month of the year to you" (Ex. 12:1–2). "This day came ye out in the month Abib" (Ex. 13:4).

The Hebrew word *abib* or *aviv* meant the time when the barley shoots into the ear (or is ripe), meaning it was ready for harvest. It is alphabetically the first word in the Hebrew dictionary. "And if thou offer a meat offering of thy firstfruits unto the LORD, thou shalt offer for the meat offering of thy firstfruits green ears of corn [*abib*] dried by the fire, even corn beaten out of full ears" (Lev. 2:14). "Thou shalt keep the feast of unleavened bread: (thou shalt eat unleavened bread seven days, as I commanded thee, in the time appointed of the month Abib; for in it thou camest out from Egypt: and none shall appear before me empty" (Ex. 23:15).

By using the barley harvest, they determined whether or not to start a new year, a holy calendar. If by the time of the new moon the barley harvest were ready to begin, they would start a new year. However, if the barley were not quite ready to harvest, they would wait to begin a new year until the next new moon. Since the barley harvest was always in sync with the solar year, this system worked quite nicely. This reckoning of months would require the addition of an additional month to some years. Of course, as the chart shows, they had a name for this additional month. So most years would have twelve months, and some years would have thirteen.

Josephus wrote the following:

> This calamity happened in the 600th year of Noah's government [age], in the second month, called by the

Macedonians Dius, but by the Hebrews Marchesuan: for so did they order their year in Egypt: but Moses appointed that Nisan, which is the same with Xanthieus, should be the first month for their festivals, because he brought them out of Egypt in that month, so that this month began the year as to all the solemnities they observed to the honour of God, although he preserved the original order of the months as to selling and buying, and other ordinary affairs.[1]

Walter Cummins explains further in *The Acceptable Year of the Lord*,

According to this first century record from Josephus, the Hebrew month Marcheshvan was the second month in the time of Noah, and thus Tishri would have been the first month and the beginning of the year before God told Moses to change the beginning of the year to Nisan. Josephus also noted that after the calendar change, which "Moses appointed," Nisan was the first month of the year with regard to Israel's festivals and other sacred matters, while Tishri was still the first month for selling, buying and other ordinary affairs, which were civil matters.[2]

The great thing about this way of reckoning months and years is that it was observable. That is to say, anyone could keep track of time by observing the barley harvest and the new moons. Once all these calendars have been reconstructed, we can look at the dates given in the Bible to see if they match up with a scientifically verifiable astronomical calendar.

Sabbath Years

The Bible speaks about "Sabbath years." We have nothing like it in our Gregorian calendar system of reckoning time. Every seventh year was a

---

[1] Josephus, *Antiquities Vol. 1*, pg. 44.
[2] Walter J. Cummins, *The Acceptable Year of the Lord* (Franklin: Scripture Counseling, 2005), 32.

Sabbath year. The word "Sabbath" means "rest." The Sabbath year was a year of rest from certain activities.

When the children of Israel entered Canaan, every seventh year was to be observed as a Sabbath year. During this year, the land was to rest, the fields were left unseeded, and the vineyards were left unpruned. God promised to provide an adequate harvest each sixth year so there would be enough produce to carry them through the Sabbath year and into the next, that is, until the next harvest.

It was also a year of remission in which creditors were instructed to cancel the debts of the poor and the slaves were to be released. In addition, the law was to be read publicly throughout the land.

Therefore, when the Bible describes a situation in which the law is being read, slaves are released, bills are paid or remitted, and the land lies idle, it is quite likely referring to a Sabbath year. This year will be a multiple of seven years from every other Sabbath year. (cf. Ex. 23:10–11; Deut. 15:1–2, 31:10–13).

Jubilee Years

God seems to love sevens. Seven days are in a week. Seven years are in a Sabbath-year cycle. Now the multiple of sevens is bumped up one more degree. Leviticus 25:8–11 says,

And thou shalt number seven sabbaths of years unto thee, seven times seven years; and the space of the seven sabbaths of years shall be unto thee forty and nine years. Then shalt thou cause the trumpet of the jubile to sound on the tenth day of the seventh month, in the day of atonement shall ye make the trumpet sound throughout all your land. And ye shall hallow the fiftieth year, and proclaim liberty throughout all the land unto all the inhabitants thereof: it shall be a jubile unto you; and ye shall return every man unto his possession, and ye shall return every man unto his family. A jubile shall that fiftieth year be unto you: ye shall not sow, neither reap that which groweth of itself in it, nor gather the grapes in it of thy vine undressed.

So Jubilee years were the seventh Sabbath years. In this year, the children of Israel were commanded to do all of the other things of a Sabbath year. Plus every farm was to be returned to its original owner.

There is some confusion as to whether Jubilee years were every forty-nine or fifty years. Suffice it to say here, the Jubilee years were separated by forty-nine years, but the forty-ninth year became the fiftieth year since the last Jubilee, counting the last Jubilee as year one.

Priestly Cycles

The children of Israel marked the passage of time in yet one more way. It had to do with the service of various groups—or sections—of priests in the temple at Jerusalem. King David instituted the priestly cycles, although he may have simply perpetuated a practice that may have reached back as far as the death of Aaron.

The priests were divided up into twenty-four sections.[3] Every Saturday a new section of priests took over the service of the temple. The priestly divisions were called the Hebrew word *mishmar*, meaning "watch." This cycle took 168 days. (7 days times 24 sections equals 168 days.) When it was completed, it started all over again, time after time.

In Luke 1:5, Zacharias was a priest, and his time to serve in the temple was after the course of Abia, which was one of the twenty-four priestly courses. "There was in the days of Herod, the king of Judaea, a certain priest named Zacharias, of the course of Abia: and his wife was of the daughters of Aaron, and her name was Elisabeth."

---

[3] For more in-depth explanation on the divisions of the priests, see 1 Chronicles 24.

Chapter 2
Appointed Times

God instituted days and weeks, months, and years. He also instituted "appointed times" or fixed periods of time frames and a "meeting place." God gave these appointed times and places to Israel, His chosen people. God set these times, not man. Let's look at what some of these appointed times and places were.

Numbers 9:2 says, "Let the children of Israel also keep the passover at his appointed season." And Leviticus 23:1–2 reads, "And the Lord spake unto Moses, saying, Speak unto the children of Israel, and say unto them, concerning the feasts of the Lord, which ye shall proclaim to be holy convocations, even these are my feasts."

The phrase "feast of the Lord" is the same word as "appointed seasons" in Numbers. It is the Hebrew word *moed*, which means a "fixed time." It is used as the time of birth or the season of migrating birds, but our focus will be specific to God's appointed times given to Israel.

God first established this word *moed* in Genesis 1:14, "And God said, Let there be lights in the firmament of the heaven to divide the day from the night; and let them be for signs, and for seasons [*moed* same word as appointed times], and for days, and years."

In chapter 1, we read that God divided the day and night. This verse says that the stars were to be used for four things: signs, seasons (appointed times), days, and years.

Psalm 104:19 also speaks of the moon as being appointed for seasons (*moed*), "He appointed the moon for seasons *moed*: the sun knoweth his going down."

God appointed seasons. He also appointed meeting places. God met with Moses at the "tent meeting" (*ohel moed*), literally meaning "the tent of appointed meeting place." It can also be translated as "appointed place." Exodus 33:7 says,

> And Moses took the tabernacle, and pitched it without the camp, afar off from the camp, and called it the Tabernacle of the congregation. And it came to pass, that every one which sought the LORD went out unto the tabernacle of the congregation, which was without the camp.

The tabernacle of congregation could also be rendered "tabernacle of meeting."

God met with Moses and spoke to him mouth to mouth, plainly saying "With him will I speak mouth to mouth, even apparently, and not in dark speeches; and the similitude of the LORD shall he behold" (Num. 12:8). The purpose of God meeting with Moses and Israel was to impart revelation.

Exodus 29:42 says, "This shall be a continual burnt offering throughout your generations at the door of the tabernacle of the congregation before the LORD: where I will meet you, to speak there unto thee." And Numbers 29:39 reads, "These things ye shall do unto the LORD in your set feasts, beside your vows, and your freewill offerings, for your burnt offerings, and for your meat offerings, and for your drink offerings, and for your peace offerings."

In this verse, "set feasts" is the same word for "appointed times."

Ezra later reestablished these feast days for the children of Israel. Ezra 3:5 says, "And afterward offered the continual burnt offering, both of the new moons, and of all the set feasts of the LORD that were consecrated, and of every one that willingly offered a freewill offering unto the LORD."

Here we see that God set *moed* (appointed times or set feasts), not man. They were the "set feasts of the Lord."

We are now going to look at a synonymous word to *moed*, the Hebrew word *miqra*. The word *miqra* is translated as "convocation, assembly, rehearsal, and invitation." *Miqra* designates the weekly Sabbaths and the new moons. The root word is *qara*, which means to "call or call out." It is used customarily to address a specific recipient and is intended to elicit a specific response. That is why it is translated "to proclaim or invite."[4]

Leviticus 23:2, 4, 7 says,

> Speak unto the children of Israel, and say unto them, Concerning the feasts of the LORD, which ye shall proclaim to be holy convocations, even these are my feasts ... These are the feasts of the Lord, even holy convocations, which ye shall proclaim in their seasons ... In the first day ye shall have an holy convocation: ye shall do no servile work therein.

And Ezekiel 46:3 reads, "Likewise the people of the land shall worship at the door of this gate before the LORD in the Sabbaths and in the new moons."

However, its most common meaning is reserved for the seven special convocation Sabbaths. Isaiah 66:23 says, "And it shall come to pass, that from one new moon to another, and from one Sabbath to another, shall all flesh come to worship before me, saith the LORD."

Such days included a formal summoning of people to worship by the blast of the trumpets. Numbers 10:2, 10 says,

> Make thee two trumpets of silver; of a whole piece shalt thou make them: that thou mayest use them for the calling of the assembly, and for the journeying of the camps ... Also in the day of your gladness, and in your solemn days, and in the beginnings of your months, ye shall blow with the trumpets over your burnt offerings, and over the sacrifices of your peace offerings; that they may be to you for a memorial before your God: I am the LORD your God.

---

[4] R. Laird Harris, ed., *Theological Wordbook of the Old Testament, Vol.2* (Chicago: Moody Press, 1980), 810–811.

Men blowing the shofar in the wilderness

God is the one who established these appointed times and seasons, and He called Israel to worship Him and to His holy feast days. We are now going to see how God directed them to "make ready" for these times.

Chapter 3
Preparations

God instructed Israel to make preparations and be ready for His coming to speak to them on Mount Sinai. He told them what things to do or not do in order for them to be prepared. Exodus 19:9–11 says,

> And the Lord said unto Moses, Lo, I come unto thee in a thick cloud, that the people may hear when I speak with thee, and believe thee for ever. And Moses told the words of the people unto the Lord. And the Lord said unto Moses, Go unto the people, and sanctify them to day and to morrow, and let them wash their clothes, And be ready against the third day: for the third day the LORD will come down in the sight of all the people upon mount Sinai.

Part of their making ready or "be ready" was to wash their clothes and abstain from coming unto their spouse. Later this making ready also included all servile work. So preparing meals, cooking unleavened bread, buying, and selling all had to be done prior to any weekly Sabbath or feast day. All these items were to be carried out. This sixth day before the weekly Sabbath and before any feast was called the "day of preparation."

God also made His own preparations for Israel. He sent an angel to go before Israel into the Promised Land and bring them to the place He had prepared. Exodus 23:20 says, "Behold, I send an Angel before thee, to keep thee in the way, and to bring thee into the place which I have prepared."

The Gospels reveal a clear understanding of these preparations. Matthew 26:17–19 reads,

> Now the first day of the feast of unleavened bread the disciples came to Jesus, saying unto him, Where wilt thou that we prepare for thee to eat the passover? And he said, Go into the city to such a man, and say unto him, The Master saith, My time is at hand; I will keep the passover at thy house with my disciples. And the disciples did as Jesus had appointed them; and they made ready the passover.

Here the disciples "made ready" for the Passover. Matthew 27:62 says, "Now the next day, that followed the day of the preparation, the chief priests and Pharisees came together unto Pilate." And Mark 14:12–16 reads,

> And the first day of unleavened bread, when they killed the passover, his disciples said unto him, Where wilt thou that we go and prepare that thou mayest eat the passover? And he sendeth forth two of his disciples, and saith unto them, Go ye into the city, and there shall meet you a man bearing a pitcher of water: follow him. And wheresoever he shall go in, say ye to the goodman of the house, The Master saith, Where is the guestchamber, where I shall eat the passover with my disciples? And he will shew you a large upper room furnished and prepared: there make ready for us. And his disciples went forth, and came into the city, and found as he had said unto them: and they made ready the passover.

Luke 22:1–6 says,

> Now the feast of unleavened bread drew nigh, which is called the Passover. And the chief priests and scribes sought how they might kill him; for they feared the people. Then entered Satan into Judas surnamed

Iscariot, being of the number of the twelve. And he went his way, and communed with the chief priests and captains, how he might betray him unto them. And they were glad, and covenanted to give him money. And he promised, and sought opportunity to betray him unto them in the absence of the multitude.

It says in verse 1 that the feast "drew nigh." The chief priests sought to betray Jesus Christ in expectation that they would accomplish this before the feast. The feast day was soon approaching. This was during the time of preparations before the feast. John 19:14 says, "And it was the preparation of the passover, and about the sixth hour: and he saith unto the Jews, Behold your King!"

Let's look at Matthew a bit more closely. Matthew 26:17 reads, "Now the first day of the feast of unleavened bread the disciples came to Jesus, saying unto him, Where wilt thou that we prepare for thee to eat the Passover?"

We have a problem right here in this verse. It says it was "the first day of the feast of unleavened bread." The feast of unleavened bread was the day **after** the Passover, yet it says the disciples were asking Jesus about preparing for the Passover. All their preparations for Passover would have been done prior to Passover. They would have secured a location, made their purchases, precooked or prepared all the food, and cleaned out their house of leaven. It was popular for children to help by making it a fun game. Everything would have been made ahead of time. A more accurate rendering of this verse would be, "Now the feast of unleavened bread was nigh or coming near."

In Mark 14:12, the same problem occurs. "And the first day of unleavened bread, when they killed the passover, his disciples said unto him, Where wilt thou that we go and prepare that thou mayest eat the passover?"

In translating these verses, the Greeks did not fully understand the details of Israel's feasts. The Passover lamb was killed on Passover, the fourteenth of Nisan, and the Feast of Unleavened Bread started the next day. (See Exodus 12:1–20.) God established this with Moses. This next day was a high holy Sabbath, starting the beginning of the Feast of

Unleavened Bread, which lasted eight days. At the time of Jesus Christ's crucifixion, the fourteenth of Nisan was on a Wednesday. Thursday was the high holy Sabbath, and Saturday was the weekly Sabbath.

Luke 22:1 has the correct translation. "Now the feast of unleavened bread drew nigh, which is called the Passover."

Let's read from John in context about the timing of Pilate bringing Jesus out. John 19:13–14 says,

> When Pilate therefore heard that saying, he brought Jesus forth, and sat down in the judgment seat in a place that is called the Pavement, but in the Hebrew, Gabbatha. And it was the preparation of the passover, and about the sixth hour: and he saith unto the Jews, Behold your King!

From our study so far, we know it was the preparation day and the sixth hour. That would be the day before Passover at noon. Once you understand God's appointed times and the feast days, whole sections of God's Word become clearer.

A further explanation is given in Appendix 156, "Six Days Before the Passover" (John 12:1), in E. W. Bullinger's *The Companion Bible*.[5]

> We are furnished by Scripture with certain facts and fixed points which, taken together, enable us (1) to determine the events which filled up the days of "the last week" of our Lord's life on earth; (2) to fix the day of His crucifixion; and (3) to ascertain the duration of the time He remained in the tomb.
>
> The difficulties connected with these three have arisen (1) from not having noted these fixed points; (2) from the fact of Gentiles' not having been conversant with the law concerning the three great feasts of the LORD; and (3) from not having reckoned the days as commencing (some six hours before our own) and

---

[5] E. W. Bullinger, *The Companion Bible* (Grand Rapids: Zondervan, 1974), 179.

running from sunset to sunset, instead of from midnight to midnight.

To remove these difficulties, we must note:—

I. That the first day of each of the three feasts. Passover, Pentecost, and Tabernacles, was "a holy convocation", a "sabbath" on which no servile work was to be done. See Leviticus 23:7, 24, 35. Compare Exodus 12:16.

"That sabbath" and the "high day" of John 19:31, was the "holy convocation", the first day of the feast, which quite overshadowed the ordinary weekly sabbath.

It was called by the Jews Yom tov = (Good day), and this is the greeting on that day throughout Jewry down to the present time.

This great sabbath, having been mistaken from the earliest times for the weekly sabbath, has led to all the confusion.

II. This has naturally caused the futher difficulty as to the Lord's statement that "even as Jonah was in the belly of the fish three days and three nights, so shall the Son of man be in the heart of the earth three days and three nights" (Matthew 12:40). Now, while it is quite correct to speak according to Hebrew idiom of "three days" or "three years", while they are only parts of three days or three years, yet that idiom does not apply in a case like this, where "three nights" are mentioned in addition to "three days." It will be noted that the Lord not only definitely states this, but repeats the full phraseology, so that we may not mistake it.

One of the important things in preparation for these feast days was to purify themselves.[6] John 11:55 says, "And the Jews' passover was nigh

---

[6] Laws concerning purification are Leviticus 7:21, Numbers 19:11–22, and Numbers 31:19–24.

at hand: and many went out of the country up to Jerusalem before the passover, to purify themselves."

Ceremonial cleanness can be seen in Jesus's time by whitewashing sepulchers and to avoid them. Even Pharisees took measures to stay pure. John 18:28 says, "Then led they Jesus from Caiaphas unto the hall of judgment: and it was early; and they themselves went not into the judgment hall, lest they should be defiled; but that they might eat the passover."

Another practical preparation for the Feast of the Passover was the selection of the lamb that was to take place on the tenth of Nisan. Exodus 12:3–6 reads,

> Speak ye unto all the congregation of Israel, saying, In the tenth day of this month they shall take to them every man a lamb, according to the house of their fathers, a lamb for an house: And if the household be too little for the lamb, let him and his neighbour next unto his house take it according to the number of the souls; every man according to his eating shall make your count for the lamb. Your lamb shall be without blemish, a male of the first year: ye shall take it out from the sheep, or from the goats: And ye shall keep it up until the fourteenth day of the same month: and the whole assembly of the congregation of Israel shall kill it in the evening.

All preparations for Passover went on up until the time of eating the Passover meal. In Christ's time, there were many tasks for these preparations. The Greek word *paraskeve*, which means "preparations," can be one day prior to a feast or span over several days prior to a feast (for example, thanksgiving preparations).

Mark 15:42 says, "And now when the even was come, because it was the preparation, that is, the day before the Sabbath." Luke 23:54 reads, "And that day was the preparation, and the sabbath drew on." And John 19:14 states, "And it was the preparation of the passover, and about the sixth hour: and he saith unto the Jews, Behold your King!"

The sixth hour was noon, the same time the lamb was being slain in the final hours before the Passover began. Verse 31 says, "The Jews therefore, because it was the preparation, that the bodies should not remain upon the cross on the sabbath day, (for that sabbath day was an high day,) besought Pilate that their legs might be broken, and that they might be taken away."

They broke the legs of those crucified to hasten their deaths so they could be taken away and buried. Verse 42 reads, "There laid they Jesus therefore because of the Jews' preparation day; for the sepulchre was nigh at hand."

Laws concerning purification are Numbers 19:11–22, 31:19–2 and Leviticus 7:21.

To summarize, for the three annual feasts that required all males to attend, there were many preparations to be carried out: from the blowing of the trumpets announcing the feast; preparing for their journeys to Jerusalem, including fixing roads for the travelers; and making sure they were ceremonially clean to being mentally and spiritually prepared.[7]

---

[7] James M. Freeman, *Manners and Customs of the Bible* (Plainfield: Logo International, 1972), 70.

Chapter 4
Passover in the Old Testament

Much has been written about Passover, probably more than any other feast day of the Old Testament. Yet it is very misunderstood among many Christians today.

I would like to start by pointing out what Passover is *not* in this day and time for the Christian church. It is not the celebration of the Last Supper or communion. It is not the celebration of Easter, although they coincide with our modern calendar. It is not the Messianic Haggadah, which several Christian churches participate in.

The word *haggadah* means "the telling," but the root word means "to keep a feast or celebrate a holiday." It actually refers to the three main pilgrimages-feasts of Israel. Passover was also not the recrucifying of Christ.

So what is Passover to the church today? First, let us review what Passover was to Israel, Exodus 12:1–14. Verses 1 and 2 say, "And the Lord spake unto Moses and Aaron in the land of Egypt saying, This month shall be unto you the beginning of months [Abib or Nisan, our March/April]: it shall be the first month of the year to you."

Then verses 3 and 4 read,

> Speak ye unto all the congregation of Israel, saying, In the tenth day of this month [4 days before Passover] they shall take to them every man a lamb [they were to groom the lamb], according to the house of their fathers, a lamb for an house: And if the household be too little for the lamb, let him and his neighbor next unto his house take it

according to the number of the souls; every man according to his eating shall make your count for the lamb.

Finally verses 5 through 14 say,

Your lamb shall be without blemish, a male of the first year: ye shall take it out from the sheep, or from the goats: [without blemish and of the first year, not three years]. And ye shall keep it (keep the lamb was part of the preparation) up until the fourteenth day of the same month: and the whole assembly of the congregation of Israel shall kill it in the evening. And they shall take of the blood, and strike it on the two side posts and on the upper door post of the houses, wherein they shall eat it. And they shall eat the flesh in that night, roast with fire, and unleavened bread; and with bitter herbs they shall eat it. Eat not of it raw, nor sodden at all with water, but roast with fire; his head with his legs, and with the purtenance thereof. And ye shall let nothing of it remain until the morning; and that which remaineth of it until the morning ye shall burn with fire. And thus shall ye eat it; with your loins girded, your shoes on your feet, and your staff in your hand; and ye shall eat it in haste: it is the Lord's passover. [Christ was sitting down at the last supper, in Passover they ate standing up in haste]. For I will pass through the land of Egypt this night, and will smite all the firstborn in the land of Egypt, both man and beast; and against all the gods of Egypt I will execute judgment: I am the Lord. And the blood shall be to you for a token upon the houses where ye are: and when I see the blood, I will pass over you, and the plague shall not be upon you to destroy you, when I smite the land of Egypt. And this day shall be unto you for a memorial; and ye shall keep it a feast to the Lord throughout your generations; ye shall keep it a feast by an ordinance for ever.

God instituted Passover. It was to be a memorial of God delivering them out of the hands of Egypt. God established this feast by saying it twice. Anytime God mentions something twice, it means it is established, "ye shall **keep it a feast** to the Lord throughout your generations; **ye shall keep it a feast** by an ordinance for ever."

Exodus 12:26–28 says,

> And it shall come to pass, when your children shall say unto you, What mean ye by this service? That ye shall say, It is the sacrifice of the Lord's Passover, who passed over the houses of the children of Israel in Egypt, when he smote the Egyptians, and delivered our houses. And the people bowed the head and worshipped. And the children of Israel went away, and did as the Lord had commanded Moses and Aaron, so did they.

Three things set the Passover date. It was to be on the fourteenth of Nisan or Abib, which was the first month. The first month was established by the sighting of the new moon, and the barley had to be *abib* (ripe to harvest), "as I commanded you in the appointed time in the month of abib, for in the month abib you came out of Egypt."[8]

Abib was the Old Testament name of the first month of the sacred calendar, while Nisan is a more modern name. The sighting of the new moon and the barley harvest being ripe had to have two witnesses who would come to the temple and give testimony of both occurrences. Then the priest would announce the beginning of the first month by having them blow the trumpets. The day following Passover started the Feast of Unleavened Bread, which lasted seven days.

---

[8] New King James Version, Exodus 34:18b.

Israels's Annual Feasts				
Feast Name	Month of the Sacred Year	Day	Males Required to Attend	Corresponding Month
Passover	1 - Abib	14	Yes	March-April
Ex. 12:1-14; Lev. 23:5; Num. 9:1-14, 28:16; Deut. 16:1-7				
Unleavened Bread	1 - Abib	15-21	Yes	March-April
Ex. 12:15-20; 13:3-10; Lev. 23:6-8; Num. 28:17-25; Deut. 16:3,4,8				
Firstfruits (Wave Offering)	1 - Abib and		No	March-April May-June
Lev. 23:9-14; Num. 28:26 - First day after the weekly Sabbath during the Feast of Unleavened bread.				
Weeks (Harvest or Pentecost)	3 - Sivan	50 days after	Yes	May-June
Ex. 23:16, 34:22; Lev. 23:15-21; Num. 28:26-31; Deut. 16:9-12 - Start the counting on the wave offering day.				
Trumpets (Rosh Hashanah)	7 - Tishri	1	No	September-October
Lev. 23:23-25; Num.29:1-6				
Day of Atonement (Yom Kippur)	7 - Tishri	10	No	September-October
Lev. 16; 23:26-32; Num. 29:7-11				
Tabernacles (Booths or Ingathering)	7 - Tishri	15-22	Yes	September-October
Ex 23:16, 34:22; Lev. 23:33-36, 39-43; Num. 29:12-38; Deut. 16:13-15				
The Last Great Day - High Sabbath on the last day of the Feast of Tabernacles				

The Passover was to be a memorial of God passing over the Israelites' homes while in Egypt, not allowing the destroyer to strike them (Ex. 12:23). No stranger was allowed to partake in the Passover unless he was first circumcised (Ex. 12:43–51). They were also told to eat the Passover standing up (Ex. 12:11). This is contrary to Jesus and the disciples sitting down to eat the Last Supper.

Now we will look at how Passover relates to the church today in the New Testament. Passover today is called Rosh HaShannah, which literally means "head of the year." The Jews today call the Passover meal a "Passover seder."

Chapter 5
What Does Passover Mean to the Church Today?

The word "passover" is only used two times in the church epistles: once in the book of Hebrews referring to Moses's faith and the other time in 1 Corinthians referring to Christ as being our Passover.

Hebrews 11:28 says, "Through faith he [Moses] kept the Passover, and the sprinkling of blood, lest he that destroyed the firstborn should touch them." And 1 Corinthians 5:7 reads, "Purge out therefore the old leaven, that ye may be a new lump, as ye are unleavened. For even Christ our Passover is sacrificed for us."

The King James Version reads the verse as "is sacrificed," but it should be in the past tense since it has already been accomplished and completed. The Aramaic translation reads "for our Passover (figure of speech ellipsis, add [Lamb]) is Christ, who was sacrificed on our behalf."

Magiera defines an ellipsis as "words omitted from a sentence or phrase that are necessary to complete the grammar, but not the sense."[9] The New King James Version translates this, "For indeed Christ, our Passover, was sacrificed for us." Hebrews 10:1 says, "For the law having a shadow of good things to come, and not the very image of the things, can never with those sacrifices which they offered year by year continually make the comers thereunto perfect."

These feast days were foreshadows of things to come. All of these sacrificial offerings that were done either daily, weekly, or yearly could not perfect a person. Hebrews 10:2–4, says,

---

[9] Janet M. Magiera, *Aramaic Peshitta New Testament Translation* (Truth or Consequences: LWMP Publications, 2006), 399, 604.

For then would they not have ceased to be offered? because that the worshippers once purged should have had no more conscience of sins. But in those sacrifices there is a remembrance again made of sins every year. For it is not possible that the blood of bulls and of goats should take away sins.

And verses 5–7 reads,

Wherefore when he cometh into the world, he saith, Sacrifice and offering thou wouldest not, but a body hast thou prepared me. In burnt offerings and sacrifices for sin thou hast had no pleasure. Then said I, Lo, I come (in the volume of the book it is written of me,) to do thy will, O God. [This is a quote from Psalm 40:6–8].

These sacrifices did not fulfill God's ultimate desire. They were mere **shadows of things to come**. God's will was that these sacrifices should be fulfilled in the offering of the body of Jesus Christ. Hebrews 10:8–14 reads,

Above when he said, Sacrifice and offering and burnt offerings and offering for sin thou wouldest not, neither hadst pleasure therein; which are offered by the law; Then said he, Lo, I come to do thy will, O God. He taketh away the first, that he may establish the second. By the which will we are sanctified through the offering of the body of Jesus Christ once for all. And every priest standeth daily ministering and offering oftentimes the same sacrifices, which can never take away sins: But this man, after he had offered one sacrifice for sins for ever, sat down on the right hand of God; [the completed work]. From henceforth expecting till his enemies be made his footstool. For by one offering he hath perfected for ever them that are sanctified.

Today the church has no reason to keep this feast day. The Passover was to be remembered as a completed work of Jesus Christ. This final offering by Jesus Christ was done **once** and for all, never to be done again. This man (Christ) offered himself, one sacrifice for sins forever, and sat down at the right hand of God. Sitting down represents the completed work, just as God sat when He finished His creation and rested. Jesus Christ **was** the Passover past tense and completed work, a new covenant.

Chapter 6
The Feast of Unleavened Bread

We saw that Christ is our Passover, "For even Christ our Passover is sacrificed for us" (1 Cor. 5:7). It is a completed work, and He has sat down at the right hand of God. Let's go back to 1 Corinthians 5 and read the context about Passover and the Feast of Unleavened Bread. First Corinthians 5:1 sets the context, "It is reported commonly that there is fornication among you, and such fornication as is not so much as named among the Gentiles, that one should have his father's wife."

Paul addresses the concerns about sexual immorality. The Corinthians were puffed up to the point they were glorying in it. Paul was trying to teach them "to deliver such a person to Satan for the destruction of the flesh, that the spirit may be saved" (verse 5).

We need to spiritually discern situations that need purging. The church needs to purge out the evil amongst them. This is why it says in verse 6, "Your glorying is not good, know ye not that a little leaven leavens the whole lump?"

Leaven was used in making bread. It was made originally from fine white bran; kneaded with must from the meal of certain plants (such as fitch, vetch, or barley); mixed with water; and then allowed to stand until it turned sour. As baking developed, leaven was produced from the bread flour kneaded without salt and kept until it passed into a state of fermentation.[10]

Exodus 34:18 says, "The feast of unleavened bread shalt thou keep.

---

[10] J. D. Douglas, *The New Bible Dictionary* (Grand Rapids: Wm. B. Eerdmans Publishing, 1962), 725.

Seven days thou shalt eat unleavened bread, as I commanded thee, in the time of the month Abib: for in the month Abib thou camest out from Egypt."

Leaven was prohibited to be used at the time of Passover and the Feast of Unleavened Bread.[11] The Feast of Unleavened Bread was to remind Israel of the bread of haste when they left Egypt in a hurry. They did not have time to wait for the bread to rise. The feast was also called the "bread of affliction."

The feast lasted seven days and had a high holy Sabbath on the first and last day. The showbread that was used in the temple was also made without leaven. Leviticus 10:12 says, "And Moses spake unto Aaron, and unto Eleazar and unto Ithamar, his sons that were left, Take the meat offering that remaineth of the offerings of the LORD made by fire, and eat it without leaven beside the altar: for it is most holy."

In the Gospels, Jesus Christ uses the word "leaven" figuratively, meaning "corrupt or corrupting." Matthew 16:6 says, "Then Jesus said unto them, Take heed and beware of the leaven of the Pharisees and of the Sadducees." And Mark 8:15 reads, "And he charged them, saying, Take heed, beware of the leaven of the Pharisees, and of the leaven of Herod."

Jesus warns of the leaven of both the Pharisees and the Herodians. Mark 3:6 says, "And the Pharisees went forth, and straightway took counsel with the Herodians against him, how they might destroy him." Pharisees represented the religious leaders, and the Herodians were the political leaders.

Matthew 13:33 reads, "Another parable spake he unto them; The kingdom of heaven is like unto leaven, which a woman took, and hid in three measures of meal, till the whole was leavened."

This parable is speaking about the kingdom of heaven. "The hiding of the leaven till the whole was leavened" is in reference to the idea that the kingdom of heaven is still growing. The consummation will be

---

[11] See Exodus 23:18 and 34:25: "Thou shalt not offer the blood of my sacrifice with leavened bread; neither shall the fat of my sacrifice remain until the morning … Thou shall not offer the blood of my sacrifice with leaven; neither shall the sacrifice of the feast of the Passover be left unto the morning."

realized at the end of ages. Paul says to purge out the old leaven. He was referring to the corruption and lies that crept into the church.

First Corinthians 5:7–8 reads, "Purge out therefore the old leaven, that ye may be a new lump, as ye are unleavened. For even Christ our passover is sacrificed for us: Therefore let us keep the feast, not with old leaven, neither with the leaven of malice and wickedness; but with the unleavened bread of sincerity and truth."

We truly are unleavened, the lively bread (Word of God) we are sustained with. We live this Word with sincerity and truth, not malice or wickedness. In verse 7, it says we are unleavened, which means we are pure with no contaminates. In verse 8, Paul encourages us to keep the Feast of Unleavened Bread. Is he saying we should go back to Old Testament law? No, we saw earlier that we cannot keep the Feast of Passover because Jesus Christ was the Passover (past tense). Christ fulfilled that and brought in a new covenant. But Paul is saying to keep the Feast of Unleavened Bread. What does he mean here?

We are to keep this feast with sincerity and truth. The word "sincerity" is the Greek word *eilikrineia* and means "to be clearly judged by sunlight." In the Oriental bazaars (markets) where pottery was sold, some merchants would show their wares in poorly lit rooms. Unscrupulous merchants would try to sell patched or fractured pottery. But a savvy buyer would hold up a piece to the sunlight to see if there were any flaws.

Paul also makes reference to leaven in Galatians. Galatians 5:8–10 says, "This persuasion cometh not of him that calleth you. A little leaven leaveneth the whole lump. I have confidence in you through the Lord, that ye will be none otherwise minded: but he that troubleth you shall bear his judgment, whosoever he be."

Paul was dealing with these religious Christians who were trying to bring a yoke of bondage on the Galatians. Just as Jesus Christ warned the disciples about the leaven of the Pharisees (the religious leaders in that day) and the Herodians (the political leaders in Jerusalem), so Paul warns of those who want to be religious and have fallen away from the liberty and grace that we have in Christ. There were many religious leaders who were born again but brought the old ways with them. Paul encouraged them to stand fast in this liberty and to walk in sincerity and truth.

Chapter 7
The Eighteenth of Nisan, The Wave Offering

During the Feast of Unleavened Bread, the day after the first regular weekly Sabbath, was the presentation of the wave offering. The wave offering was the beginning of the counting toward Pentecost fifty days later (also known as the Feast of Weeks). The wave offering was originally called the Firstfruits of the Barley Harvest. This was the beginning of the spring harvest.

Leviticus 23:9–15 says,

> And the Lord spake unto Moses, saying, Speak unto the children of Israel, and say unto them, When ye be come into the land which I give unto you, and shall reap the harvest thereof, then ye shall bring a sheaf of the firstfruits of your harvest unto the priest: And he **shall wave the sheaf before the Lord**, to be accepted for you: **on the morrow after the sabbath the priest shall wave it**. And ye shall offer that day when ye wave the sheaf an he lamb without blemish of the first year for a burnt offering unto the Lord. And the meat offering thereof shall be two tenth deals of fine flour mingled with oil, an offering made by fire unto the Lord for a sweet savour: and the drink offering thereof shall be of wine, the fourth part of an hin. And ye shall eat neither bread, nor parched corn, nor green ears, until the selfsame day that ye have brought an offering unto your God: it shall be a statute for ever throughout your generations in all your

> dwellings. And ye shall count unto you from the morrow
> after the sabbath, from the day that ye brought the sheaf
> of the wave offering; seven sabbaths shall be complete:

The wave offering foreshadowed Jesus Christ as the firstfruits from the dead. Christ's resurrection was on the eighteenth of Nisan. It was His first day in His resurrected body. Let us read from John 20. John 20:1 says, "The first day of the week cometh Mary Magdalene early, when it was yet dark, unto the sepulchre, and seeth the stone taken away from the sepulchre."

It was the first day of the week, the day after the weekly Sabbath. Mary Magdalene was the first one to arrive at the sepulcher. Then the disciples arrived but later went away to their home, and Mary remained at the sepulcher weeping. John 20:15–16 reads,

> Jesus saith unto her, Woman, why weepest thou? whom seekest thou? She, supposing him to be the gardener, saith unto him, Sir, if thou have borne him hence, tell me where thou hast laid him, and I will take him away. Jesus saith unto her, Mary. She turned herself, and saith unto him, Rabboni; which is to say, Master.

She had mistaken Jesus for a gardener in verse 15, but in the next verse, it says that Jesus revealed Himself to her. And John 20:17 reads, "Jesus saith unto her, Touch me not; for I am not yet ascended to my Father: but go to my brethren, and say unto them, I ascend unto my Father, and your Father; and to my God, and your God."

Jesus told Mary not to touch Him because He was the firstfruits from the dead. The wave offering of the firstfruits, in which the spring barley harvest were presented as an offering to God, was to occur that same day. Jesus Christ replaced that offering as the true firstfruits from the dead.[12]

---

[12] Victor Paul Wierwille, *Jesus Christ Our Passover* (New Knoxville: American Christian Press, 1981), 320.

Rabboni

First Corinthians 15:20, 23 says, "But now is Christ risen from the dead, and become the firstfruits of them that slept … But every man in his own order: Christ the firstfruits; afterwards they that are Christ's at his coming." And Acts 26:23 reads, "That Christ should suffer, and that he should be the first that should rise from the dead, and should shew light unto the people, and to the Gentiles."

On this day, the priest presenting the offering would go up to the temple to present it before the Lord. That is the meaning of the expression, "I ascend unto my Father, and your Father; unto my God, and your God." Psalms 120 through 134 were titled "A Song of Ascents." They were sung by pilgrims ascending the hills to Jerusalem for the yearly feasts. Christ would go up and, as the high priest, present Himself before God as the firstfruits from the dead. It does not, however, refer to the ascension to heaven, which was yet forty days away. [13]

In preparing to present Himself as the firstfruits, Christ would, in accordance with Old Testament law, keep Himself separated until it was accomplished. In the law, priests were to cleanse themselves at the brass laver of water between the tabernacle of the congregation and the altar before going in the holy place. [14]

Exodus 30:17–21 says,

> And the Lord spake unto Moses, saying, Thou shalt also make a laver of brass, and his foot also of brass, to wash withal: and thou shalt put it between the tabernacle of the congregation and the altar, and thou shalt put water therein. For Aaron and his sons shall wash their hands and their feet thereat: When they go into the tabernacle of the congregation, they shall wash with water, that they die not; or when they come near to the altar to minister, to burn offering made by fire unto the Lord: So they shall wash their hands and their feet, that they die not: and it shall be a statute for ever to them, even to him and to his seed throughout their generations.

According to Leviticus, the priest had to be holy when presenting offerings to God (Lev. 21:6).[15] No priest could handle or partake of the holy offerings unless he was ceremonially pure, meaning, among other things, he had not touched anyone who could legally be considered

---

[13] Wierwille, *Jesus Christ Our Passover*, 320.
[14] Ibid.
[15] Ibid., 320–321.

unclean (Lev. 22:1–9). In addition, the priest could not have any blemish on him (Lev. 21:17–24). In Exodus, the brazen laver filled with water was also used for the priest to see if he had any blemishes on him by looking at his reflection in the water (Ex. 38:8).

The wave offering of the firstfruits was a public offering, meaning the priest on behalf of the nation of Israel performed it. Therefore, a priest would maintain a state of purity before bringing the offering before the Lord at the temple. Besides being Himself the firstfruits offering, Jesus Christ was also the priest making the offering. He was showing Himself as the true High Priest of Israel.[16]

Hebrews 5:5–6 says, "So also Christ glorified not himself to be made an high priest; but he that said unto him, Thou art my Son, to day have I begotten thee. As he saith also in another place, Thou art a priest for ever after the order of Melchisedec." And Hebrews 8:1 reads, "Now of the things which we have spoken this is the sum: We have such an high priest, who is set on the right hand of the throne of the Majesty in the heavens."

Jesus Christ presented Himself to many of the disciples as well as the apostles, openly demonstrating He was the firstfruits from the dead. "To whom also he shewed himself alive after his passion by many infallible proofs, being seen of them forty days, and speaking of the things pertaining to the kingdom of God" (Acts 1:3).

This new body He had was pretty remarkable. Let's take a look at some of what this new body could do:

- Mary mistook Him as a gardener. "Jesus saith unto her, Woman, why weepest thou? whom seekest thou? She, supposing him to be the gardener" (John 20:15a).
- He appeared in another form. "After that he appeared in another form unto two of them, as they walked, and went into the country" (Mark 16:12).
- He appeared to the eleven at mealtime. "Afterward he appeared unto the eleven (as Simon was not present) as they sat at meat" (Mark 16:14).

[16] Ibid., 321.

- They saw Him but did not recognize him. "But their eyes were holden that they should not know him" (Luke 24:16).
- Then their eyes were opened, and He vanished. Wow! "And their eyes were opened, and they knew him; and he vanished out of their sight" (Luke 24:31).
- He appeared suddenly to Simon. "Saying, The Lord is risen indeed, and hath appeared to Simon" (Luke 24:34).
- Suddenly He stood in the midst of them. They were terrified, thinking He was a spirit. "And as they thus spake, Jesus himself stood in the midst of them, and saith unto them, Peace be unto you. But they were terrified and affrighted, and supposed that they had seen a spirit" (Luke 24:36–37).
- He spoke to them, asking, "Why are ye troubled? And why do thoughts arise in your hearts?" (Luke 24:38).
- He changed His form back to the crucified Christ and said, "Handle me and see." You can't grab on to a spirit, but He had flesh and bones, and He asked for some food to eat. This new body is awesome! It is flesh and bones. It can eat, change form, vanish, or appear instantly. "Behold my hands and my feet, that it is I myself: handle me, and see; for a spirit hath not flesh and bones, as ye see me have" (Luke 24:39).
- In John 20:20, this is where they got their spiritual 20/20 vision. He showed them His hands and His side, and they saw. "And when he had so said, he shewed unto them his hands and his side. Then were the disciples glad, when they saw the Lord."
- About eight days later, He appeared again to the disciples behind closed doors. So this new body can go through other objects (John 20:26).

In John 21, He showed Himself again to the disciples at the sea of Tiberias. John 21:1–6 reads,

> After these things Jesus shewed himself again to the disciples at the sea of Tiberias; and on this wise shewed he himself. There were together Simon Peter, and Thomas called Didymus, and Nathanael of Cana in

Galilee, and the sons of Zebedee, and two other of his disciples. Simon Peter saith unto them, I go a fishing. They say unto him, We also go with thee. They went forth, and entered into a ship immediately; and that night they caught nothing. But when the morning was now come, Jesus stood on the shore: but the disciples knew not that it was Jesus. Then Jesus saith unto them, Children, have ye any meat? They answered him, No. And he said unto them, Cast the net on the right side of the ship, and ye shall find. They cast therefore, and now they were not able to draw it for the multitude of fishes.

He was standing on the shore while Peter and a few disciples were out fishing, but they "knew not that it was Jesus." They were not so far from land that they could not hear him. In verse 8, it says two hundred cubits from shore. Jesus said, "Children, have you any meat?" And they answered no. Jesus said, "Cast the net on the right side of the ship." And then they were not able to draw it up because of the multitude of fish. One of the disciples perceived that it was the Lord. Then Peter dove in swimming with haste.

Jesus was already sitting on the shore with a little fire going and some fish and bread on the coals. Did you ever wonder where He got those fish and bread? In verse 12, they knew it was He in the minds and hearts. John 21:12–14 says,

> Jesus saith unto them, Come and dine. And none of the disciples durst ask him, Who art thou? knowing that it was the Lord. Jesus then cometh, and taketh bread, and giveth them, and fish likewise. This is now the third time that Jesus shewed himself to his disciples, after that he was risen from the dead.

These words "shewed" in verse 1 and again in verse 14 are from the Greek word *phainos*. The root word is *phos*, which means "light or to shine." It is also translated as "appeared" in Luke 24:34 and in Mark 16:12, 14.

Jesus Christ appeared in His shiny new body to all the disciples during forty days. This is what we have to look forward to when He comes back to get us. Philippians 3:20–21 reads,

> For our conversation [dwelling] is in heaven; from whence also we look for the Saviour, the Lord Jesus Christ: Who shall change our vile body, that it may be fashioned like unto his glorious body, according to the working whereby he is able even to subdue all things unto himself.

We have seen how Jesus Christ has completed every detail of fulfilling our salvation and accomplishing the requirements that were prophesied of Him. His first duty was to be that high priest after the order of Melchizedek by presenting Himself as the wave offering, which being the firstfruits from the dead.

If there were first fruits, then there will be second fruits and so on. So we have this hope that in Christ we shall all be raised from the dead, whether being asleep or alive at the time of His return. First Corinthians 15:48–55 says,

> As is the earthy, such are they also that are earthy: and as is the heavenly, such are they also that are heavenly. And as we have borne the image of the earthy, we shall also bear the image of the heavenly. Now this I say, brethren, that flesh and blood cannot inherit the kingdom of God; neither doth corruption inherit incorruption. Behold, I shew you a mystery; We shall not all sleep, but we shall all be changed, In a moment, in the twinkling of an eye, at the last trump: for the trumpet shall sound, and the dead shall be raised incorruptible, and we shall be changed. For this corruptible must put on incorruption, and this mortal must put on immortality. So when this corruptible shall have put on incorruption, and this mortal shall have put on immortality, then shall

be brought to pass the saying that is written, Death is swallowed up in victory. O death, where is thy sting? O grave, where is thy victory?

Praise God.

Chapter 8
Pentecost, The Feast of Weeks

Before we consider what Pentecost was in the New Testament, we will look at what the Feast of Pentecost was during the Old Testament times.

Pentecost in the Old Testament

Pentecost was one of the three main feast days of the Lord. It was also known as the Feast of Weeks or Spring Harvest. It was fifty days after they began to count from the first barley harvest on the day of the wave offering. Leviticus 23:15–16 says,

> And ye shall count unto you from the morrow after the sabbath, from the day that ye brought the sheaf of the wave offering; seven sabbaths shall be complete: Even unto the morrow after the seventh sabbath shall ye number fifty days; and ye shall offer a new meat offering unto the Lord.

The Hebrew name for Pentecost was *Shavuot*. In Greek, it is called Pentecost, meaning "fifty." In Exodus, it was known as "the firstfruits of thy labors," and in Numbers, it was known as "the day of the firstfruits." Exodus 23:16 says, "And the feast of harvest, the firstfruits of thy labours, which thou hast sown in the field: and the feast of ingathering, which is in the end of the year, when thou hast gathered in thy labours out of the field."

There were two harvest times: one in the beginning of the year and the other at the end. In Virginia, we used to cut hay in early June and again the second time in late August/ early September.

Numbers 28:26 says, "Also in the day of the firstfruits, when ye bring a new meat offering unto the Lord, after your **weeks** be out, ye shall have an holy convocation; ye shall do no servile work."

The background of Pentecost is in Exodus 19. According to the *Mishna* (writings of the Jewish oral traditions), the law was given to Israel on Mount Sinai on *Shavuot* (Pentecost) in written and spoken form. Exodus 19:1–2 says,

> In the third month, when the children of Israel were gone forth out of the land of Egypt, the same day came they into the wilderness of Sinai. For they were departed from Rephidim, and were come to the desert of Sinai, and had pitched in the wilderness; and there Israel camped before the mount.

Verse 1 states that the children of Israel arrived at Sinai "in the third month." Shortly thereafter, probably the same month, the law was given.

Exodus 19:3–6 says,

> And Moses went up unto God, and the LORD called unto
> him out of the mountain, saying, Thus shalt thou say to
> the house of Jacob, and tell the children of Israel; Ye
> have seen what I did unto the Egyptians, and how I bare
> you on eagles' wings, and brought you unto myself. Now
> therefore, if ye will obey my voice [*qowl*] indeed, and
> keep my covenant, then ye shall be a peculiar treasure
> unto me above all people: for all the earth is mine: And
> ye shall be unto me a kingdom of priests, and an holy
> nation. These are the words which thou shalt speak unto
> the children of Israel.

God delivered Israel from Egypt. He uses the endearing term "I
bare you on eagles' wings." If they would obey His voice and keep His
covenant, they would be a special treasure, a kingdom of priests and a
holy nation.

This word "voice" in the Hebrew is *qowl*, pronounced like our
English word "call" and is defined as "a sound produced by the vocal
chords" (actual or figuratively).[17] The first occurrence of this word is in
Genesis, "And they heard the voice of the LORD God walking in the
garden in the cool of the day" (Gen. 3:8a).

Verses 7–9 reads,

> And Moses came and called for the elders of the people,
> and laid before their faces all these words which the Lord
> commanded him. And all the people answered together,
> and said, All that the Lord hath spoken we will do. And
> Moses returned the words of the people unto the Lord.
> And the LORD said unto Moses, Lo, I come unto thee
> in a thick cloud, that the people may hear when I speak
> with thee, and believe thee for ever. And Moses told the
> words of the people unto the LORD.

---

[17] R. Laird Harris, ed., *Theological Wordbook of the Old Testament, Vol. 2*, 792.

So Moses told the elders and the people what God had said, and they all agreed. God wanted to talk to all the people of Israel, not just Moses, "that the **people** may hear when I speak."

Verses 10–11 reads, "And the LORD said unto Moses, Go unto the people, and sanctify them to day and to morrow, and let them wash their clothes, And be ready against the third day: for the third day the LORD will come down in the sight of all the people upon mount Sinai."

They were to wash and sanctify themselves to be pure. This was their preparation time to get ready. Every feast day and Sabbath they made ready. This preparation is also known as rehearsals, an invitation. God invited them to come to the foot of the mountain, and He was going to speak to them there.

Verses 12 and 13 says,

> And thou shalt set bounds unto the people round about, saying, Take heed to yourselves, that ye go not up into the mount, or touch the border of it: whosoever toucheth the mount shall be surely put to death: There shall not an hand touch it, but he shall surely be stoned, or shot through; whether it be beast or man, it shall not live: when the trumpet soundeth long, they shall come up to the mount.

Here God has set limits and boundaries and for them to wait for the cue to come up at the sounding of the trumpet. Verses 16–25 reads,

> And it came to pass on the third day in the morning, that there were thunders [*qowl*] and lightnings, and a thick cloud upon the mount, and the voice [*qowl*] of the trumpet exceeding loud; so that all the people that was in the camp trembled. And Moses brought forth the people out of the camp to meet with God; and they stood at the nether part of the mount. And mount Sinai was altogether on a smoke, because the LORD descended upon it in fire: and the smoke thereof ascended as the smoke of a furnace, and the whole mount quaked greatly.

And when the voice *[qowl]* of the trumpet sounded long, and waxed louder and louder, Moses spake, and God answered him by a voice *[qowl]*. And the LORD came down upon mount Sinai, on the top of the mount: and the LORD called Moses up to the top of the mount; and Moses went up. And the LORD said unto Moses, Go down, charge the people, lest they break through unto the LORD to gaze, and many of them perish. And let the priests also, which come near to the LORD, sanctify themselves, lest the LORD break forth upon them. And Moses said unto the LORD, The people cannot come up to mount Sinai: for thou chargedst us, saying, Set bounds about the mount, and sanctify it. And the LORD said unto him, Away, get thee down, and thou shalt come up, thou, and Aaron with thee: but let not the priests and the people break through to come up unto the LORD, lest he break forth upon them. So Moses went down unto the people, and spake unto them.

God wanted to talk to all the people of Israel. Keep this in mind as we begin to understand what Pentecost is all about. This Hebrew word *qowl*, meaning "voice," is used five times in this record, and in verse 16, it is used for "thunder." The people got ready for God coming to talk to them. God descended on the mountain in fire.

Deuteronomy 4:9–14 says,

Only take heed to thyself, and keep thy soul diligently, lest thou forget the things which thine eyes have seen, and lest they depart from thy heart all the days of thy life: but teach them thy sons, and thy sons' sons; Specially the day that thou stoodest before the Lord thy God in Horeb, when the Lord said unto me, Gather me the people together, and I will make them hear my words, that they may learn to fear me all the days that they shall live upon the earth, and that they may teach their children. And ye came near and stood under the mountain; and the mountain burned with fire unto the midst of heaven, with darkness, clouds, and thick darkness. And the Lord spake unto you out of the midst of the fire: ye heard the voice of the words, but saw no similitude; only ye heard a voice. And he declared unto you his covenant, which he commanded you to perform, even ten commandments; and he wrote them upon two tables of stone. And the Lord commanded me at that time to teach you statutes and judgments, that ye might do them in the land whither ye go over to possess it.

We will see many parallels to this event on Mount Sinai as we compare it to the outpouring of the holy spirit in Acts on the day of Pentecost.

Pentecost in the New Testament

Let us now tie this to the New Testament. This is the record of the Mount Transfiguration. Luke 9:27–36 reads,

But I tell you of a truth, there be some standing here, which shall not taste of death, till they see the kingdom of God. And it came to pass about an eight days after these sayings, he took Peter and John and James, and went up into a mountain to pray. And as he prayed, the fashion of his countenance was altered, and his raiment was white and glistering. And, behold, there talked with him two men, which were Moses and Elias: Who appeared in glory, and spake of his decease which he should accomplish at Jerusalem. But Peter and they that were with him were heavy with sleep: and when they were awake, they saw his glory, and the two men that stood with him. And it came to pass, as they departed from him, Peter said unto Jesus, Master, it is good for us to be here: and let us make three tabernacles; one for thee, and one for Moses, and one for Elias: not knowing what he said. While he thus spake, there came a cloud, and overshadowed them: and they feared as they entered into the cloud. And there came a voice out of the cloud, saying, This is my beloved Son: hear him. And when the **voice** was past, Jesus was found alone. And they kept it close, and told no man in those days any of those things which they had seen.

This word for "voice" is the Greek word *phonee*. It is the same word used in the Septuagint (the Greek translation of the Old Testament) for voice (*qowl*) in the Old Testament. God has always wanted to speak to His people. Acts 2:1–4 says,

And when the day of Pentecost was fully come, they were all with one accord in one place. And suddenly there came a sound from heaven as of a rushing mighty wind, and it filled all the house where they were sitting. And there appeared unto them cloven tongues like as of fire, and it sat upon each of them. And they were all filled with the Holy Ghost, and began to speak with other tongues, as the Spirit gave them utterance.

And verse 6 reads, "Now when this was noised abroad, the multitude came together, and were confounded, because that every man heard them speak in his own language."

This word "noised abroad" is this same word *phonee*. In verse 3, "cloven tongues like as of fire" descended on them. This parallels to God descending down with fire on Mount Sinai to speak to the children of Israel.

Once an individual is born again and receives the holy spirit, he now has a way to communicate to God and God has a way to communicate to him. First Corinthians talks about speaking in tongues and what it is. First Corinthians 14:2–7 says,

For he that speaketh in an unknown tongue **speaketh not unto men, but unto God**: for no man understandeth him; howbeit in the spirit **he speaketh mysteries**. But he that prophesieth speaketh unto men to edification, and exhortation, and comfort. He that speaketh in an unknown tongue **edifieth himself**; but he that prophesieth edifieth the church. I would that ye all spake with tongues but rather that ye prophesied: for greater is he that prophesieth than he that speaketh with tongues, except he interpret, that the church may receive edifying. Now, brethren, if I come unto you speaking with tongues, what shall I profit you, except I shall speak to you either by revelation, or by knowledge, or by prophesying, or by doctrine? And even things without life giving **sound**, whether pipe or harp, except they give a distinction in the **sounds**, how shall it be known what is piped or harped?

This word "sound" is the same Greek word *phonee*. What English word do you think we have that is similar? Phone! God has so been waiting to make a phone call to you and for you to talk to Him.

In the book of Hebrews, we have a summary of the first Pentecost and present day. Hebrews 12:18–26 reads,

For ye are not come unto the mount that might be touched, and that burned with fire, nor unto blackness, and darkness, and tempest, And the sound of a trumpet, and the voice of words; which voice they that heard intreated that the word should not be spoken to them any more: (For they could not endure that which was commanded, And if so much as a beast touch the mountain, it shall be stoned, or thrust through with a dart: And so terrible was the sight, that Moses said, I exceedingly fear and quake:) But **ye** [you and I] are come unto mount Sion, and unto the city of the living God, the heavenly Jerusalem, and to an innumerable company of angels, To the general assembly and church of the firstborn, which are written in heaven, and to

God the Judge of all, and to the spirits of just men made perfect, And to Jesus the mediator of the new covenant, and to the blood of sprinkling, that speaketh better things than that of Abel. See that ye refuse not him that speaketh. For if they escaped not who refused him that spake on earth, much more shall not we escape, if we turn away from him that speaketh from heaven: Whose voice then shook the earth: but now he hath promised, saying, Yet once more I shake not the earth only, but also heaven.

The word "voice" is the same Greek word, *phonee*. God has always wanted to talk to us. Just as God spoke on the Mount of Transfiguration saying, "This is my beloved son," so He says "this is my beloved son" to everyone who is born again. Speaking in tongues is the witness of this.

Second Peter 1:16–19 says,

For we have not followed cunningly devised fables, when we made known unto you the power and coming of our Lord Jesus Christ, but were eyewitnesses of his majesty. For he received from God the Father honour and glory, when there came such a voice to him from the excellent glory, This is my beloved Son, in whom I am well pleased. And this voice which came from heaven we heard, when we were with him in the holy mount. We have also a more sure word of prophecy; whereunto ye do well that ye take heed, as unto a light that shineth in a dark place, until the day dawn, and the day star arise in your hearts:

This more sure word of prophecy was the manifestations of holy spirit. Hebrews 2:4 says, "God also bearing them witness, both with signs and wonders, and with divers miracles, and gifts of the Holy Ghost, according to his own will?"

So we have seen that, on the first Pentecost, God gave them the law and wanted to speak to them. They later refused to have God speak to them; rather they chose Moses to be their intermediary (Ex. 20:18–19; Deut. 18:16–17). But after Christ's completed work, it was available for anyone to receive holy spirit and be able to have a two-way conversation with God.

In closing, let's go to 1 Corinthians 12, where is listed all nine manifestations of the holy spirit. First Corinthians 12:7–11 reads,

> But the manifestation of the Spirit is given to every man to profit withal. For to one is given by the Spirit the word of wisdom; to **another** the word of knowledge by the same Spirit; To **another** faith by the same Spirit; to **another** the gifts of healing by the same Spirit; To **another** the working of miracles; to **another** prophecy; to **another** discerning of spirits; to **another** divers kinds of tongues; to **another** the interpretation of tongues: But all these worketh that one and the selfsame Spirit, dividing to every man severally as he will.

The word "another" in these verses are two Greek words, *heteros* and *allos*. The Greek word *heteros* means "other of a different kind." *Allos* means "other of the same kind." The word *allos* is used with the manifestations "faith" and "speaking in tongues." This is because they are done between you and God only. All the rest are for the church. When you speak in tongues, it is a conversation between you and God.

Chapter 9
The Feast of Trumpets

The Feast of Trumpets, also known as Rosh Hashanah in modern day, means "memorial of blowing" in Hebrew. It was in the seventh month (Tishri) and lasted for one day during the Old Testament times, two days in modern times. This was also one of the feast days that was not mandatory for all males to attend.

Leviticus 23:24 says, "Speak unto the children of Israel, saying, In the seventh month, in the first day of the month, shall ye have a sabbath, a memorial of blowing of trumpets, an holy convocation."

It was also called Yom Teruah, literally meaning "day of blowing." Numbers 29:1 says, "And in the seventh month, on the first day of the month, ye shall have an holy convocation; ye shall do no servile work: it is a day of blowing the trumpets unto you."

The seventh month was the Hebrew month Tishri and was the commencement of the New Year. It was also the time when they coroneted kings. Old rabbinical tradition said Tishri 1 was the first day of creation.[18]

Psalm 81:3–4 says, "Blow up the trumpet in the new moon, in the time appointed, on our solemn feast day. For this was a statute for Israel, and a law of the God of Jacob."

---

[18] Victor Paul Wierwille, *Jesus Christ Our Promised* Seed (New Knoxville: American Press, 1983), 77.

Ezekiel 33 was read on this day as a reminder to warn the people. Ezekiel 33:2–6 reads,

> Son of man, speak to the children of thy people, and say unto them, When I bring the sword upon a land, if the people of the land take a man of their coasts, and set him for their watchman: If when he seeth the sword

come upon the land, he blow the trumpet, and warn
the people; Then whosoever heareth the sound of the
trumpet, and taketh not warning; if the sword come, and
take him away, his blood shall be upon his own head. He
heard the sound of the trumpet, and took not warning;
his blood shall be upon him. But he that taketh warning
shall deliver his soul. But if the watchman see the sword
come, and blow not the trumpet, and the people be not
warned; if the sword come, and take any person from
among them, he is taken away in his iniquity; but his
blood will I require at the watchman's hand.

Theodor Gaster, an American biblical scholar in the nineteenth
century, said in *Festivals of the Jewish Year* that it was a symbolic time
when "the dead return to rejoin their descendants at the beginning of
the year." Such a day was a time when Israel would rally to the call of
God for the inauguration of God's kingdom on earth.[19] The blowing
of trumpets was also the sign that kings could then begin to rule. (See
also 2 Kings 9:13 and 11:11–14.) First Kings 1:34 says, "And let Zadok the
priest and Nathan the prophet anoint him there king over Israel: and
blow ye with the trumpet, and say, God save king Solomon."

Psalm 81 said to blow the trumpets in the new moon. It should
also be noted that, in Numbers 10:10, they blew the trumpets at the
beginning of each month, at the beginning of each solemn feast day,
and over the burnt offering and peach offerings.

Numbers 10:10 states,

Also in the day of your gladness, and in your solemn
days, and in the beginnings of your months, ye shall
blow with the trumpets over your burnt offerings, and
over the sacrifices of your peace offerings; that they may
be to you for a memorial before your God: I am the Lord
your God.

[19] "The Star of Bethlehem," Chapter 6, ASK, http://www.askelm.com/star/star008.htm

According to Alfred Edersheim, "During the whole of New Year's day [Tishri 1], trumpets and horns were blown in Jerusalem from morning to evening. The Sovereignty of God is a dominant theme of the occasion [and] it is one of the cardinal features of New Year's Day."

Gaster states in *Festivals of the Jewish Year*, "Furthermore, the scholars believe that Psalms 47, 93, 96, 97 and 99—especially those psalms beginning with "the Lord [Jehovah] reigneth—were an important part of the ancient Tishri 1 celebrations."[20]

The Hebrews believed on the Day of Trumpets that God rules overall and He is the King of Kings. On the Feast of Trumpets, it was common to quote Zechariah 14:16ff because it pointed toward the upcoming Feast of Tabernacles.

The central theme of the Day of Trumpets is clearly that of the enthronement of the great King of Kings. The Day of Trumpets in the Jewish calendars is New Year's Day for civil and royal reckonings, just as we have January 1 on our Roman calendar as the start of our New Year. This New Year's Day signified a time of "new beginnings" to all those in Israel. As a matter of fact, the Jews over the centuries have held to the belief that the Day of Trumpets was a cardinal date in the history of Adam.

Wierwille writes on the significance of Tishri 1 in his book *Jesus Christ our Promised Seed*,

> The association of the blowing of a trumpet with kingship is also made in the Book of Revelation. Revelation 8:2 speaks of the seven angels with seven trumpets. The first six angels blow their trumpets in Revelation 8:6, 7, 8, 10, 12; 9:1 and 13. Finally, the seventh angel sounds the trumpet.

Revelation 11:15–17:

> And the seventh angel sounded; and there were great voices in heaven, saying, The kingdoms of this world are become the kingdoms of our Lord, and of his Christ; and he shall reign for ever and ever.

---

[20] Wierwille, *Jesus Christ Our Promised Seed*, 79–81.

And the four and twenty elders, which sat before God
on their seats, fell upon their faces, and worshipped God,

Saying, We give thee thanks, O Lord God Almighty,
which art, and wast, and art to come; because thou hast
taken to thee thy great power, and hast reigned.

The purpose of the introductory crescendo of the first
six trumpets leading up to the sounding of the seventh
was to bring complete attention to the sovereignty of
God. That it was the seventh trumpet that sounded is
highly significant. Recall that the first of each month,
beginning with Nisan, was to be observed with the
blowing of trumpets. But Tishri 1 was the seventh new
moon, the beginning of the seventh month, and the great
Day of Trumpets. As this was a time of blowing trumpets
and of celebrating the lordship of Jehovah in the Old
Testament, so the seventh trumpet in Revelation will
herald the lordship of God and His Son. Thus, Tishri 1
with the blowing of the trumpets noted the birth of the
King of Kings. What an appropriate and notable day for
Jesus Christ to have been born! What perfect alignment
of history when we consider that Jesus Christ was born
on Tishri 1, New Year's Day of Adam's reckoning. It
was the first day of the seventh month, the last festal
month of Moses' calendar. It was the day beginning the
regnal years of the kings of Judah. It was the great Day
of Trumpets celebrating Jehovah as the one True God.

On that very day, Tishri 1, September 11, 3 B.C.,
Jesus Christ, God's only begotten Son, was born in
Bethlehem. Unknown to the people, the trumpet sounds
which blew from morning to evening in Jerusalem
heralded God as the King overall and His Son as the
promised king under the King, God. Yes, the Messiah,
the promised seed, the second Adam, had been born.[21]

---

[21] Ibid., 81–83.

Let's look at Numbers to further see the description of the trumpets themselves and how they were to be used. Numbers 10:1–10 says,

> And the LORD spake unto Moses, saying, Make thee two trumpets of silver; of a whole piece shalt thou make them: that thou mayest use them for the calling of the assembly, and for the journeying of the camps. And when they shall blow with them, all the assembly shall assemble themselves to thee at the door of the tabernacle of the congregation. And if they blow but with one trumpet, then the princes, which are heads of the thousands of Israel, shall gather themselves unto thee. When ye blow an alarm, then the camps that lie on the east parts shall go forward. When ye blow an alarm the second time, then the camps that lie on the south side shall take their journey: they shall blow an alarm for their journeys. But when the congregation is to be gathered together, ye shall blow, but ye shall not sound an alarm. And the sons of Aaron, the priests, shall blow with the trumpets; and they shall be to you for an ordinance for ever throughout your generations. And if ye go to war in your land against the enemy that oppresseth you, then ye shall blow an alarm with the trumpets; and ye shall be remembered before the LORD your God, and ye shall be saved from your enemies. Also in the day of your gladness, and in your solemn days, and in the beginnings of your months, ye shall blow with the trumpets over your burnt offerings, and over the sacrifices of your peace offerings; that they may be to you for a memorial before your God: I am the LORD your God.

There were three types of trumpets Israel used: the *shofar*, a ram's horn; the *hasosra*, also known as the *chatsotserah*; and the *qeren*, a cornet used in Babylon.

In the temple, the two *chatsotserahs* were placed with a *shofar* in the middle of them. They were blown for four reasons: war, praise, direction, and gathering together.

It is interesting to note that God descended on Mount Sinai with a loud trump and that Paul describes Christ coming back to gather us together with the voice of the archangel and the trump of God. Next we are going to look at the Day of Atonement.

Chapter 10
The Day of Atonement

The time between the Feast of Trumpets and the Day of Atonement was called "the ten days of awe." It was also called "the ten days of preparation" and a time of reflection. In modern times, it is called Yom Kippur, "time of judgment." God spoke to Moses in Leviticus 23. Leviticus 23:26–32 reads,

> And the LORD spake unto Moses, saying, Also on the tenth day of this seventh month there shall be a day of atonement: it shall be an holy convocation unto you; and ye shall afflict your souls, and offer an offering made by fire unto the LORD. And ye shall do no work in that same day: for it is a day of atonement, to make an atonement for you before the LORD your God. For whatsoever soul it be that shall not be afflicted in that same day, he shall be cut off from among his people. And whatsoever soul it be that doeth any work in that same day, the same soul will I destroy from among his people. Ye shall do no manner of work: it shall be a statute for ever throughout your generations in all your dwellings. It shall be unto you a sabbath of rest, and ye shall afflict your souls: in the ninth day of the month at even, from even unto even, shall ye celebrate your sabbath.

The Day of Atonement was the only day of the year that the high priest would go into the Holy of Holies and offer incense for the whole nation of Israel. It was the wrongdoing of Aaron's sons (Nadab and Abihu) who took strange fire, brought it before the Lord, and, as a result, died. Because of Aaron's sons, God told Moses to tell Aaron that they were not to come in to the Holy of Holies at just any time. God told Moses to speak to Aaron saying, "I will be sanctified in them that come nigh me, and before all the people I will be glorified. And Aaron held his peace" (Lev. 10:1–3).

In Leviticus 16, God instructs Moses to tell Aaron how he is to come into the holy place (with an offering, wearing linen, and after washing his flesh with water). Leviticus 16:2–4 reads,

> And the Lord said unto Moses, Speak unto Aaron thy brother, that he come not at all times into the holy place within the vail before the mercy seat, which is upon the ark; that he die not: for I will appear in the cloud upon the mercy seat. Thus shall Aaron come into the holy place: with a young bullock for a sin offering, and a ram for a burnt offering. He shall put on the holy linen coat, and he shall have the linen breeches upon his flesh, and shall be girded with a linen girdle, and with the linen mitre shall he be attired: these are holy garments; therefore shall he wash his flesh in water, and so put them on.

The context of Leviticus 16 is about the cleansing of Aaron and the priests. God is holy and cannot allow contamination (James 1:13; Lev. 11:44–45). This cleansing of the priests and the temple is a foreshadowing of Christ cleansing the church. Ephesians 5:24–27 states,

> Therefore as the church is subject unto Christ, so let the wives be to their own husbands in every thing. Husbands, love your wives, even as Christ also loved the church, and gave himself for it; That he might sanctify and cleanse it with the washing of water by the word, That he might present it to himself a glorious church, not having spot, or wrinkle, or any such thing; but that it should be holy and without blemish.

This "washing" is a direct parallel to the washing of the priests in the bronze laver.

In *Manners and Customs of the Bible*, Freeman writes regarding Leviticus 16:34, "And this shall be an everlasting statute unto you, to make an atonement for the children of Israel for all their sins once a year. And he did as the Lord commanded Moses."

> The Great Day of Atonement took place on the tenth day of the seventh month, Tishri, corresponding to our October. It was a day of great solemnity, especially designed and kept as a fast day, (see Leviticus 23:27; Numbers 29:7; compare Psalm 35:13; Isaiah 58:5) and in later times was known by the name of The Fast, Acts 27:9. On this day the high priest, clad in plain white linen garments, brought for himself a young bullock for a sin offering and a ram for a burnt-offering; and for the people two young goats for a sin-offering, and a ram for a burnt-offering. The two goats were brought before the door of the Tabernacle, and by the casting of lots one was designated for sacrifice and the other for a scape-goat. The high priest then slaughtered the bullock and made a sin-offering for himself and family. He next entered the Most Holy Place for the first time, bearing a censer with burning coals, with which he filled the place with incense. Taking the blood of the slain bullock, he entered the Most Holy Place the second time, and there sprinkled the blood before the mercy-seat. He next killed the goat which was for the people's sin-offering, and, entering the Most Holy Place the third time, sprinkled its blood as he had sprinkled that of the bullock. Some of the blood of the two animals was then put on the horns of the alter of incense, and sprinkled on the alter itself. After this the high priest, putting his hands on the head of the scape-goat, confessed the sins of the people, and then sent him off into the wilderness. He then washed himself, and changed his garmets, arraying himself in the beautiful

robes of his high office, and offered the two rams as burn-offerings for himself and for the people. (Leviticus 16:34)[22]

On the Day of Atonement, every forty-nine years was "the Year of Jubilee."

Leviticus 25:8–10 says,

> And thou shalt number seven sabbaths of years unto thee, seven times seven years; and the space of the seven sabbaths of years shall be unto thee forty and nine years. Then shalt thou cause the trumpet of the jubile to sound on the tenth day of the seventh month, in the day of atonement shall ye make the trumpet sound throughout all your land. And ye shall hallow the fiftieth year, and **proclaim liberty** throughout all the land unto all the inhabitants thereof: it shall be a jubile unto you; and ye shall return every man unto his possession, and ye shall return every man unto his family.

Compare this with what Jesus Christ read from Luke 4:18-19,this is quoted from Isaiah. Isaiah 61:1–2 reads,

> The Spirit of the Lord GOD is upon me; because the LORD hath anointed me to preach good tidings unto the meek; he hath sent me to bind up the brokenhearted, to **proclaim liberty** to the captives, and the opening of the prison to them that are bound; To proclaim the acceptable year of the LORD.

Some believe that Jesus Christ read this aloud in the synagogue of Nazareth on the Day of Atonement and that it was also the Year of Jubilee. This feast, as with the Feast of Trumpets, was not mandatory for all males to attend.[23] John 7:2 and 8–10 states,

---

[22] Freeman, *Manners and Customs of the Bible*, 91.

[23] See appendix 7 on the chronological timeline of Jesus Christ.

> Now the Jew's feast of tabernacles was at hand … Go
> ye up unto this feast: I go not up yet unto this feast: for
> my time is not yet full come. When he had said these
> words unto them, he abode still in Galilee. But when his
> brethren were gone up, then went he also up unto the
> feast, not openly, but as it were in secret.

What feast were they talking about? As we have seen with the Feast of Trumpets and the Feast of Atonement, men were not required to attend these. Jesus's brethren decided to go attend these feasts, but Jesus abode in Galilee. That is why He could recite Isaiah 61 on the Day of Atonement in Nazareth. He later joined them at the Feast of Tabernacles because that was a required feast day for all males to attend.

How does this feast day apply to the church today? Only the high priest could enter the Holy of Holies once a year, but because of what Jesus Christ accomplished, we can enter into God's presence because we have been sanctified. A parallel to the Day of Atonement can be found in the book of Hebrews. Hebrews 10:19–22 says,

> Having therefore, brethren, boldness to enter into the
> holiest by the blood of Jesus, By a new and living way,
> which he hath consecrated for us, through the veil, that
> is to say, his flesh; And having an high priest over the
> house of God; Let us draw near with a true heart in full
> assurance of faith, having our hearts sprinkled from an
> evil conscience, and our bodies washed with pure water.

In *Jesus Christ our Approach Offering*, David Bergey writes:

> On the Day of Atonement as the high priest entered,
> his body was washed with water (Leviticus 16:4b) and
> the blood of the sin offering was sprinkled (Leviticus
> 16:11 and 14). When Hebrews 10:22 says we are to draw
> near," … having our hearts sprinkled from an evil
> conscience, and our bodies washed with pure water,"
> this is a direct reference to the Day of Atonement.

Although Hebrews never used the exact words "Day of Atonement," time and time again this most important day in the Old Testament is referenced. The Paramount theme of Hebrews is entering into God's presence, and it was exclusively on that day that the entry into the holy of holies occurred.

These phrases in Hebrews 10:22 express New Covenant realities in Old Covenant terminology. These Old Testament acts are used to describe what Christ has accomplished for us in the new birth. The two main symbols of cleansing and purification of the Old Covenant were sprinkling with the blood of the sin offering, and the washing of water. Both are mentioned here to express the utter totality of our purity by the blood of Christ.[24]

Remember what God said to Moses about Aaron's sons, that no one could approach God who was impure or unclean. Because of what Christ accomplished for us, we now have access directly into God's presence. We have been sanctified and made holy by the blood of Jesus.

Ephesians 1:4 says, "According as he hath chosen us in him before the foundation of the world, that we should be holy and without blame before him in love."

---

[24] David Bergey, *Jesus Christ our Approach Offering* (David Bergey, 2004), 127.

Chapter 11
The Feast of Tabernacles

As we saw, Tishri 1 was the beginning of the civil calendar, and it was also the Feast of Trumpets. Ten days later was the Day of Atonement. Then five days later was the Feast of Tabernacles, also called Feast of Ingatherings. In modern day, it is called Sukkot, which means "booths or tents." This feast was also called the Feast of Tents. It was seven days long with an additional eighth day as a high holy day called "The Last Great Day." The Feast of Tabernacles was to remind Israel of their sojourning in the wilderness, and God sojourned with them in His own tent or tabernacle. Here is what God spoke to Moses about this feast. Leviticus 23:33–44 says,

> And the LORD spake unto Moses, saying, Speak unto the children of Israel, saying, The fifteenth day of this seventh month shall be the feast of tabernacles for seven days unto the LORD. On the first day shall be an holy convocation: ye shall do no servile work therein. Seven days ye shall offer an offering made by fire unto the LORD: on the eighth day shall be an holy convocation unto you; and ye shall offer an offering made by fire unto the LORD: it is a solemn assembly; and ye shall do no servile work therein. These are the feasts of the LORD, which ye shall proclaim to be holy convocations, to offer an offering made by fire unto the LORD, a burnt offering, and a meat offering, a sacrifice, and drink offerings, every thing upon his day: vows, and beside

all your freewill offerings, which ye give unto the LORD. Also in the fifteenth day of the seventh month, when ye have gathered in the fruit of the land, ye shall keep a feast unto the LORD seven days: on the first day shall be a sabbath, and on the eighth day shall be a sabbath. And ye shall take you on the first day the boughs of goodly trees, branches of palm trees, and the boughs of thick trees, and willows of the brook; and ye shall rejoice before the LORD your God seven days. And ye shall keep it a feast unto the LORD seven days in the year. It shall be a statute for ever in your generations: ye shall celebrate it in the seventh month. Ye shall dwell in booths seven days; all that are Israelites born shall dwell in booths: That your generations may know that I made the children of Israel to dwell in booths, when I brought them out of the land of Egypt: I am the LORD your God. And Moses declared unto the children of Israel the feasts of the LORD.

This was one of the main feast days that all males were to attend. They were to do no servile work and offer specific offerings, and after they had gathered the fruit of the land, they were to gather trees, branches, and willows to remind them that God made them to dwell in booths when He brought them out of Egypt.

One of the things that God wanted for Israel was for them to rejoice before the Lord. Deuteronomy 16:13–15 says,

> Thou shalt observe the feast of tabernacles seven days,
> after that thou hast gathered in thy corn and thy wine:
> And thou shalt rejoice in thy feast, thou, and thy son, and
> thy daughter, and thy manservant, and thy maidservant,
> and the Levite, the stranger, and the fatherless, and the
> widow, that are within thy gates. Seven days shalt thou
> keep a solemn feast unto the LORD thy God in the place
> which the LORD shall choose: because the LORD thy God
> shall bless thee in all thine increase, and in all the works
> of thine hands, **therefore thou shalt surely rejoice.**

God says, "Thou shalt surely rejoice." The word to "rejoice" is not used in the Feast of Passover or Unleavened Bread. It is used once in Pentecost. But for the Feast of Tabernacles, it is used several times. "Rejoice" is the Hebrew word *samach*, and it means "to be glad, be joyful, be merry." It is considered one of the main praise words.[25] In the book of Nehemiah, it says there was very great gladness on keeping this feast. Nehemiah 8:13–18 says,

> And on the second day were gathered together the chief
> of the fathers of all the people, the priests, and the
> Levites, unto Ezra the scribe, even to understand the
> words of the law. And they found written in the law
> which the LORD had commanded by Moses, that the
> children of Israel should dwell in booths in the feast of
> the seventh month: And that they should publish and

---

[25] For further insight, see appendix 4, "Rejoice Before the Lord."

proclaim in all their cities, and in Jerusalem, saying, Go forth unto the mount, and fetch olive branches, and pine branches, and myrtle branches, and palm branches, and branches of thick trees, to make booths, as it is written. So the people went forth, and brought them, and made themselves booths, every one upon the roof of his house, and in their courts, and in the courts of the house of God, and in the street of the water gate, and in the street of the gate of Ephraim. And all the congregation of them that were come again out of the captivity made booths, and sat under the booths: for since the days of Jeshua the son of Nun unto that day had not the children of Israel done so. And there was **very great gladness**. Also day by day, from the first day unto the last day, he read in the book of the law of God. And they kept the feast seven days; and on the eighth day was a solemn assembly, according to the prescribed manner.

There are several parallels and foreshadows with this feast that points to the hope. For Israel, it was the hope of a New Jerusalem and a permanent home. The Feast of Tabernacles was considered the greatest of all the feasts of the year. It was the fall harvest, and Israel rejoiced at how God had blessed them in providing for them. It represented the times of restored fellowship with the Lord. It also represented God dwelling among His redeemed people (Ex. 29:44–46). This is to be fulfilled in Revelation 11:15–19.

When Christ comes to reign on earth (the millennial reign), all nations will come to Jerusalem to keep the Feast of Tabernacles. Zechariah 14:16–21 reads,

And it shall come to pass, that every one that is left of all the nations which came against Jerusalem shall even go up from year to year to worship the King, the LORD of hosts, and to keep the feast of tabernacles. And it shall be, that whoso will not come up of all the families of the earth unto Jerusalem to worship the King, the LORD of hosts, even upon them shall be no rain. And if the family of Egypt go not up, and come not, that have no rain; there shall be the plague, wherewith the LORD will smite the heathen that come not up to keep the feast of tabernacles. This shall be the punishment of Egypt, and the punishment of all nations that come not up to keep the feast of tabernacles. In that day shall there be upon the bells of the horses, HOLINESS UNTO THE LORD; and the pots in the LORD's house shall be like the bowls before the altar. Yea, every pot in Jerusalem and in Judah shall be holiness unto the LORD of hosts: and all they that sacrifice shall come and take of them, and seethe therein: and in that day there shall be no more the Canaanite in the house of the LORD of hosts.

Isaiah also prophesied of this. Isaiah 2:2–3 says,

And it shall come to pass in the last days, that the mountain of the Lord's house shall be established in the top of the mountains, and shall be exalted above the hills; and all nations shall flow unto it. And many people shall go and say, Come ye, and let us go up to the mountain of the Lord, to the house of the God of Jacob; and he will teach us of his ways, and we will walk in his paths: for out of Zion shall go forth the law, and the word of the Lord from Jerusalem.

It was the last of the three pilgrimages to Jerusalem made by all males. In the Feast of Tabernacles, the whole feast pointed toward the hope by using imagery of tents and booths that were temporary dwelling places. During this feast, Israel would make booths out of branches, which they collected to remind them of their time of wandering in the desert. One of the main concepts of this feast day is God wanting to dwell with His people. For Israel, it was the reminder that they looked to a New Jerusalem and a temple not made with hands.

Acts 7:44–50 reads,

Our fathers had the tabernacle of witness in the wilderness, as he had appointed, speaking unto Moses, that he should make it according to the fashion that he had seen. Which also our fathers that came after brought in with Jesus into the possession of the Gentiles, whom God drave out before the face of our fathers, unto the days of David; Who found favour before God, and desired to find a tabernacle for the God of Jacob. But Solomon built him an house. Howbeit the most High dwelleth not in temples made with hands; as saith the prophet, Heaven is my throne, and earth is my footstool: what house will ye build me? saith the Lord: or what is the place of my rest? Hath not my hand made all these things?

This fulfillment is further explained in Revelation 21. Revelation 21:1–7 states,

And I saw a new heaven and a new earth: for the first heaven and the first earth were passed away; and there was no more sea. And I John saw the holy city, new Jerusalem, coming down from God out of heaven, prepared as a bride adorned for her husband. And I heard a great voice out of heaven saying, Behold, the tabernacle of God is with men, and he will dwell with them, and they shall be his people, and God himself shall be with them, and be their God. And God shall wipe away all tears from their eyes; and there shall be no more death, neither sorrow, nor crying, neither shall there be any more pain: for the former things are passed away. And he that sat upon the throne said, Behold, I make all things new. And he said unto me, Write: for these words are true and faithful. And he said unto me, It is done. I am Alpha and Omega, the beginning and the end. I will give unto him that is athirst of the fountain of the water of life freely. He that overcometh shall inherit all things; and I will be his God, and he shall be my son.

This Feast of Tabernacles was also a foreshadow for the church, that we must put off this temporary dwelling place.

Second Peter 1:13–14 reads, "Yea, I think it meet, as long as I am in this tabernacle, to stir you up by putting you in remembrance; Knowing that shortly I must put off this my tabernacle, even as our Lord Jesus Christ hath shewed me."

As it says in 2 Corinthians 4:7a, "We have this treasure in earthen vessels." We look forward to getting caught up with the Lord, having a new body, and permanently dwelling with him. For God made His abode in us through Christ, God dwells in us. "But ye are not in the flesh, but in the Spirit, if so be that the Spirit of God dwell in you. Now if any man have not the Spirit of Christ, he is none of his" (Rom. 8:9).[26]

Ephesians 1:18–23 says,

> The eyes of your understanding being enlightened; that ye may know what is the hope of his calling, and what the riches of the glory of his inheritance in the saints, And what is the exceeding greatness of his power to us-ward who believe, according to the working of his mighty power, Which he wrought in Christ, when he raised him from the dead, and set him at his own right hand in the heavenly places, Far above all principality, and power, and might, and dominion, and every name that is named, not only in this world, but also in that which is to come: And hath put all things under his feet, and gave him to be the head over all things to the church, Which is his body, the fullness of him that filleth all in all.

Ephesians 2:6 reads, "And hath raised us up together, and made us sit together in heavenly places in Christ Jesus." And Ephesians 3:11–12

---

[26] For additional insight, see appendix 3, "Abide in Christ." Other references to our body being a tabernacle include 2 Corinthians 5:1–4 and John 2:19–21.

states, "According to the eternal purpose which he purposed in Christ Jesus our Lord: In whom we have boldness and access with confidence by the faith of him."

As we look at this Feast of Tabernacles, we see more and more how wonderful God's love is and His eternal purpose for both the church and Israel.

Chapter 12
The Last Great Day

The Last Great Day was the final high Sabbath that concluded the Feast of Tabernacles. Leviticus 23:36 says,

> Seven days ye shall offer an offering made by fire unto the LORD: on the eighth day shall be an holy convocation unto you; and ye shall offer an offering made by fire unto the LORD: it is a solemn assembly; and ye shall do no servile work therein.

This last day has the hope written all over it. As we saw from the previous chapter, Isaiah 2:1–3 talks about God's future house for Israel. Isaiah 2:2–4 reads,

> And it shall come to pass in the last days, that the mountain of the Lord's house shall be established in the top of the mountains, and shall be exalted above the hills; and all nations shall flow unto it. And many people shall go and say, Come ye, and let us go up to the mountain of the Lord, to the house of the God of Jacob; and he will teach us of his ways, and we will walk in his paths: for out of Zion shall go forth the law, and the word of the Lord from Jerusalem. And he shall judge among the nations, and shall rebuke many people: and they shall beat their swords into plowshares, and their

> spears into pruninghooks: nation shall not lift up sword
> against nation, neither shall they learn war any more.

The rest of Isaiah 2:5–22 talks about the "day of the Lord."[27]

This festival was on the eighth day of the Feast of Tabernacles. The number eight also had a spiritual significance, meaning "new beginning." And the Hebrew word for "eight" is related to another meaning, "fatness," implying abundance and fertility, even resurrection and regeneration. The offerings required on this day in the Old Testament were larger than that of any other feast day, typifying Israel's thankfulness to God for all He provided.

This Last Great Day foreshadows the reign of the Messiah, the prevalent conditions of the millennium—God's government, peace, prosperity, and so forth—and the Feast of Tabernacles prophesied in Zechariah 14:16–21.

There is another aspect to this day in that it foreshadows the pouring out of holy spirit as a nation. As we read earlier in Hebrews 12:18–19, Israel came to Mount Sinai, and God visited them there. Yet they refused to believe and obey His voice. They refused to have a personal conversation with God on that day.

I want to further explain how this high Sabbath day, the Last Great Day, foreshadowed the outpouring of the holy spirit. As we will see in John 7, it talks about the outpouring of the holy spirit. But first we must clear up a misunderstood verse that explains the timeline of the events in John 6–7. Not understanding John 6:4 is why so many believe that Jesus Christ's ministry lasted three years instead of one. John 6:4 states, "And the Passover, a feast of the Jews, was nigh."

There are a few reasons this feast was not Passover. The early church fathers had their own misunderstandings of this verse. Some Greek manuscripts omit John 6:4 altogether. The evidence from the early writers indicates that the word rendered "passover" in John 6:4 was not in the early manuscripts that they had.[28]

---

[27] For a more detailed explanation of the phrase "the day of the Lord," see appendix 9, "The Day of the Lord."

[28] Walter J. Cummins, *The Acceptable Year of the Lord*, 66.

But outside of the theological comments, there are other reasons from the context that it was not Passover. In verse 1, Jesus is in the Galilee area and went up on a mountain. Mosaic law required all males to be at Jerusalem for the three main feasts, Passover being one of them. Also, if it were Passover, one could not have any bread with leaven in it.

In verse 5, Phillip asks, "Whence shall we buy bread, that these may eat?" This bread referred to here is the Greek word *artos*. It was leavened bread. Unleavened bread is the Greek work *azumos*.

In the gospel of John are two astonishing records regarding the Last Great Day. Let's read this in context. Jesus Christ is still in the Galilee area around Capernaum. In verse 35 of the gospel of John, Jesus is telling them that he is the bread of life. [29] John 6:39–54 says,

> And this is the Father's will which hath sent me, that of all which he hath given me I should lose nothing, but should **raise it up again at the last day**. And this is the will of him that sent me, that every one which seeth the Son, and believeth on him, may have everlasting life: and I will **raise him up at the last day.** The Jews then murmured at him, because he said, I am the bread which came down from heaven. And they said, Is not this Jesus, the son of Joseph, whose father and mother we know? how is it then that he saith, I came down from heaven? Jesus therefore answered and said unto them, Murmur not among yourselves. No man can come to me, except the Father which hath sent me draw him: and I will **raise him up at the last day**. It is written in the prophets, And they shall be all taught of God. Every man therefore that hath heard, and hath learned of the Father, cometh unto me. Not that any man hath seen the Father, save he which is of God, he hath seen the Father. Verily, verily, I say unto you, He that believeth on me hath everlasting life. I am that bread of life. Your fathers did eat manna in the wilderness, and are dead.

[29] See appendix 5 for a full explanation of the context of John 6–7.

This is the bread which cometh down from heaven, that a man may eat thereof, and not die. I am the living bread which came down from heaven: if any man eat of this bread, he shall live for ever: and the bread that I will give is my flesh, which I will give for the life of the world. The Jews therefore strove among themselves, saying, How can this man give us his flesh to eat? Then Jesus said unto them, Verily, verily, I say unto you, Except ye eat the flesh of the Son of man, and drink his blood, ye have no life in you. Whoso eateth my flesh, and drinketh my blood, hath eternal life; and I will **raise him up at the last day.**

We see four verses referring to the last day. On the timeline, He was approaching the fall feasts. These included the Feast of Trumpets, the Day of Atonement, and the Feast of Tabernacles.

John 7:1 says the Feast of Tabernacles was at hand or nigh. In verse 10, He went up to this feast. (Luke 9:51–53 shows His determination to go to Jerusalem).[30] Then in the middle of the feast, Jesus went up to the temple to teach (John 7:14). Now to conclude this context here in verse 37, Jesus is about to say something that is very relevant to what is going on around Him on this Last Great Day.

John 7:37–39 says,

In the last day, that great day of the feast, Jesus stood and cried, saying, If any man thirst, let him come unto me, and drink. He that believeth on me, as the scripture hath said, out of his belly shall flow rivers of living water. (But this spake he of the Spirit, which they that believe on him should receive: for the Holy Ghost was not yet given; because that Jesus was not yet glorified.)

---

[30] See appendix 5, "Luke 9:51–53," for a more detailed explanation.

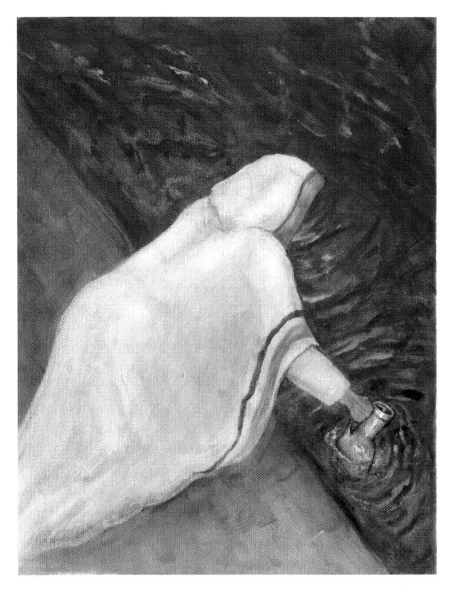

What is really happening on this Last Great Day? The people are celebrating the last day of the Feast of Tabernacles with rejoicing. The priest would come down to the pool of Siloam, dip a pitcher into the pool of water, then bring it back up to the temple, and pour it into the basins. And there is Christ crying out, "If any man thirst, let him come unto me, and drink. He that believeth on me, as the Scripture hath said, out of his belly shall flow rivers of living water."

Can you visualize this? Then it says, "But this spake he of the Spirit, which they that believe on him should receive: for the Holy Ghost was not yet given; because that Jesus was not yet glorified."

There is more to it than just what Christ spoke. He is at the pool of Siloam. Jesus is the Prince of Peace at the pool of peace on the Last Great Day, which represented Israel being at peace with God. Hosea 6:1–4 says,

> Come, and let us return unto the LORD: for he hath torn, and he will heal us; he hath smitten, and he will bind us up. After two days will he revive us: in the third day he will raise us up, and we shall live in his sight. Then shall we know, if we follow on to know the LORD: his going forth is prepared as the morning; and he shall come unto us as the rain, as the latter and former rain unto the earth. O Ephraim, what shall I do unto thee? O Judah, what shall I do unto thee? for your goodness is as a morning cloud, and as the early dew it goeth away.

Zechariah 14:8–9 reads,

> And it shall be in that day, that living waters shall go out from Jerusalem; half of them toward the former sea, and half of them toward the hinder sea: in summer and in winter shall it be. And the Lord shall be king over all the earth: in that day shall there be one Lord, and his name one.

This is what E. W. Bullinger wrote in reference to this verse from Hosea in *Figures of Speech Used in the Bible*,[31]

> But in "the last day, that great day of the feast, Jesus stood and cried," with evident reference to the Scripture

---

[31] E. W. Bullinger, *Figures of Speech Used in the Bible* (Grand Rapids: Baker Book House, 1898), 50.

which had been read, "He that believeth on me (as the Scripture hath said [*concerning Jerusalem: so shall it be*]) out of his heart rivers of living water shall flow," What the Scripture had said concerning Jerusalem in Zech. 14:8 was this: - "And it shall be in that day, *that* living waters shall go out from Jerusalem; half of them toward the former sea, and half of them toward the hinder sea," &c. To this agree the words of the prophecy in Ezek. 47:1-11. These prophecies shall yet be literally fulfilled with regard to Jerusalem: and what will then actually take place illustrates what takes place now in the experience of every one who believes in Jesus. Even as those rivers will flow forth from Jerusalem in that day, so now the Holy Spirit, in all His wondrous powers, and gifts, and graces, flows forth from the inward parts-the new nature of the believer.

On the day of Pentecost, Peter's eyes of understanding were completely opened when he quotes from Joel 2:28.

Acts 2:17–21 says,

And it shall come to pass in the last days, saith God, I will pour out of my Spirit upon all flesh: and your sons and your daughters shall prophesy, and your young men shall see visions, and your old men shall dream dreams: And on my servants and on my handmaidens I will pour out in those days of my Spirit; and they shall prophesy: And I will shew wonders in heaven above, and signs in the earth beneath; blood, and fire, and vapour of smoke: The sun shall be turned into darkness, and the moon into blood, before the great and notable day of the Lord come: And it shall come to pass, that whosoever shall call on the name of the Lord shall be saved.

Joel 2:23 reads, "Be glad then, ye children of Zion, and rejoice in the LORD your God: for he hath given you the former rain moderately, and he will cause to come down for you the rain, the former rain, and the latter rain in the first *month* [Tishri]."

Rain in this context is figuratively used for spirit. It is the former rain that is the early rain in the first month. The former rain was the spring rain; the latter rain was the fall rain. But if the civil calendar started on Tishri 1 (the New Year), then this makes sense. It is much like the rainy season in California. The early rain was the beginning of the rainy season, which started in October, and it ends in May (the late rain).

Deuteronomy 11:14 states, "That I will give you the rain of your land in his due season, the first rain and the latter rain, that thou mayest gather in thy corn, and thy wine, and thine oil."

Jeremiah also confirms this in Jeremiah 5:24. "Neither say they in their heart, Let us now fear the LORD our God, that giveth rain, both the former and the latter, in his season: he reserveth unto us the appointed weeks of the harvest."

The Last Great Day pointed to the hope and the outpouring of holy spirit. For us, we are to approach Mount Zion, not like Israel, who refused to receive God at Mount Sinai. But one day, Israel will not refuse God and will accept the outpouring of the holy spirit as a nation. Hebrews 12:18–24 says,

> For ye are not come unto the mount that might be touched, and that burned with fire, nor unto blackness, and darkness, and tempest, And the sound of a trumpet, and the voice of words; which voice they that heard intreated that the word should not be spoken to them any more: (For they could not endure that which was commanded, And if so much as a beast touch the mountain, it shall be stoned, or thrust through with a dart: And so terrible was the sight, that Moses said, I exceedingly fear and quake:) But ye are come unto mount Sion, and unto the city of the living God, the heavenly Jerusalem, and to an innumerable company of angels, To the general assembly and church of the firstborn, which are written in heaven, and to God the Judge of all, and to the spirits of just men made perfect,

And to Jesus the mediator of the New Covenant, and
to the blood of sprinkling, that speaketh better things
than that of Abel.

God called them as a chosen people, a holy nation. Here Paul refers
to two mountains. Israel was to approach Mount Sinai so God could
speak to them, yet they refused. As we saw on the day of Pentecost,
God poured out his holy spirit to those who would believe on His Son,
Jesus Christ. God always wanted to speak to His people. We, as God's
children, have approached Mount Zion. The difference is believing and
what Christ accomplished.

Micah 4:2 says,

And many nations shall come, and say, Come, and let us
go up to the mountain of the Lord, and to the house of
the God of Jacob; and he will teach us of his ways, and
we will walk in his paths: for the law shall go forth of
Zion, and the word of the Lord from Jerusalem.

Our hope is that we have a temporary dwelling now, but it will all
change when Christ comes back for us. First Corinthians 15:52 says, "In
a moment, in the twinkling of an eye, at the last trump: for the trumpet
shall sound, and the dead shall be raised incorruptible, and we shall be
changed."

Until then, we are exhorted to be patient in our waiting for Christ
to return. James 5:7–8 says,

Be patient therefore, brethren, unto the coming of the
Lord. Behold, the husbandman waiteth for the precious
fruit of the earth, and hath long patience for it, until
he receive the early and latter rain. Be ye also patient;
stablish your hearts: for the coming of the Lord draweth
nigh.

Conclusion

I would like to conclude this entire work on the feast days in 1 Peter 1:5–25.

> Blessed be the God and Father of our Lord Jesus Christ, which according to his abundant mercy hath begotten us again unto a lively hope by the resurrection of Jesus Christ from the dead, To an inheritance incorruptible, and undefiled, and that fadeth not away, reserved in heaven for you, Who are kept by the power of God through faith unto salvation ready to be revealed in the last time. Wherein ye greatly rejoice, [**as in all the feast days God wanted Israel to rejoice, so now he wants us to rejoice**] though now for a season, if need be, ye are in heaviness through manifold temptations: That the trial of your faith, being much more precious than of gold that perisheth, though it be tried with fire, might be found unto praise and honour and glory [**just as Christ showed himself in his resurrected body for forty days**] at the appearing of Jesus Christ: [**our hope**] Whom having not seen, ye love; in whom, though now ye see him not, yet believing, ye rejoice with joy unspeakable and full of glory: Receiving the end of your faith, even the salvation of your souls. Of which salvation the prophets have enquired and searched diligently, who prophesied of the grace that should come unto you: Searching what, or what manner of time the Spirit of Christ which was in them did signify, when it testified beforehand

the sufferings of Christ [**Passover**], and the glory that should follow. [**His Ascension**] Unto whom it was revealed, that not unto themselves, but unto us they did minister the things, which are now reported unto you by them that have preached the gospel unto you with the Holy Ghost sent down from heaven; [**Pentecost**] which things the angels desire to look into. Wherefore gird up the loins of your mind, be sober, and hope to the end for the grace that is to be brought unto you at the revelation of Jesus Christ; As obedient children, not fashioning yourselves according to the former lusts in your ignorance: But as he which hath called you is holy, so be ye holy [**just as Aaron and them washed in water and kept themselves clean**] in all manner of conversation; Because it is written, Be ye holy; for I am holy. [**God is Holy**] And if ye call on the Father, [**We can call we speak in tongues**] who without respect of persons judgeth [**the last great day, the white throne judgment**] according to every man's work, pass the time of your sojourning [**our temporary dwelling units Feast of Tabernacles**] here in fear: Forasmuch as ye know that ye were not redeemed with corruptible things, as silver and gold, from your vain conversation received by tradition from your fathers; But with the precious blood of Christ, as of a lamb without blemish and without spot [**Passover**] Who verily was foreordained before the foundation of the world, but was manifest in these last times for you, Who by him do believe in God, that raised him up from the dead, and gave him glory; that your faith and hope might be in God. Seeing ye have purified your souls in obeying the truth [**we are to keep the feast of Unleavened Bread with sincerity and truth**] through the Spirit unto unfeigned love of the brethren, see that ye love one another with a pure heart fervently: Being born again, not of corruptible seed, but of incorruptible, by the word of God, which liveth and abideth for ever. For all flesh is as grass, and all the glory of man as the flower of grass. The grass withereth, and the flower thereof falleth away: But the word of the Lord endureth for ever. And this is the word which by the gospel is preached unto you.

May God open your eyes of understanding to see His Word in a greater light, and let His Word anchor you. Amen.

For whatsoever things were written aforetime were written for our learning, that we through patience and comfort of the scriptures might have hope.
Romans 15:4

Appendix 1
Hebrews 10, Summary of the Feast Days

In Hebrews 10, whole sections of scriptures line up with the feast days of the Lord. All of the feast days mentioned here were a foreshadowing of **good things to come**. Most have been fulfilled in Christ. All that is left is His return, our hope. Although none of these verses mention the names of the feast days, the context gives light to them. As with all of the feast days, there were required sacrifices and offerings to be made. God instituted these sacrifices and offerings as temporary measures until His only begotten Son came to be the true and perfect sacrifice and offering.

The main theme of Hebrews is the superiority of Jesus Christ over the old covenant. One cannot truly appreciate what Jesus Christ has accomplished for us without knowing what this old covenant was. We are going to be looking at this chapter in light of how it ties into the feast days of the Old Testament.

Hebrews 10:1–14, Passover and the Feast of Unleavened Bread

In David Bergey's introduction to *Jesus Christ our Approach Offering*, he lists four basic reasons why God set up the Old Testament sacrifices.[32]

1. They reminded people of the need for a redeemer.
2. These offerings granted some limited cleansing or forgiveness of sins.

---

[32] Bergey, *Jesus Christ Our Approach Offering*, 12–13.

3. These offerings gave limited, temporary access to God.
4. God pointed out to Israel the direction from which true salvation would come.

Hebrews 10:1–5 says,

> For the law having a shadow of good things to come, and not the very image of the things, can never with those sacrifices which they offered year by year continually make the comers thereunto perfect. For then would they not have ceased to be offered? because that the worshippers once purged should have had no more conscience of sins. But in those sacrifices there is a remembrance again made of sins every year. For it is not possible that the blood of bulls and of goats should take away sins. Wherefore when he cometh into the world, he saith, Sacrifice and offering thou wouldest not, but a body hast thou prepared me: [This is talking about Christ].

This word "prepared" is the same word used in Hebrews 11:3, "framed." "The worlds were framed by the word of God." It is the Greek word *katartizo*, meaning "to arrange, set in order, equip, adjust or complete what is lacking." The word is a combination of *kata*, meaning "down," and *artizo*, meaning "complete."

Hebrews 10:6–7 says, "In burnt offerings and sacrifices for sin thou hast had no pleasure. Then said I, Lo, I come (in the volume of the book it is written of me,) to do thy will, O God."

Verses 5 through 7 are quotes from Psalm 40:6–8.

Hebrews 10:8–14 says,

> Above when he said, Sacrifice and offering and burnt offerings and offering for sin thou wouldest not, neither hadst pleasure therein; which are offered by the law; Then said he, Lo, I come to do thy will, O God. He taketh away the first, [covenant] that he may establish the second. [covenant] By the which will we are sanctified through

the offering of the body of Jesus Christ once for all. [He is our true Passover]. And every priest standeth daily ministering and offering oftentimes the same sacrifices, which can never take away sins: But this man, after he had offered one sacrifice for sins for ever, sat down on the right hand of God; [the sign of complete accomplishment] From henceforth expecting till his enemies be made his footstool. For by one offering [our Passover] he hath perfected for ever them that are sanctified.

Hebrews 10:15–18, Pentecost

In Hebrews 10:15, the subject changes from Passover to the holy spirit. "Whereof the Holy Ghost also is a witness to us: for after that he had said before, When an individual is born again and speaks in tongues, it is a witness to oneself and others that we have received the gift from God—holy spirit." And verse 16 says, "This is the covenant that I will make with them after those days, saith the Lord, I will put my laws into their hearts, and in their minds will I write them."

As we covered in chapter 8 on Pentecost, God originally gave His law to Israel on Mount Sinai. But He promised He would write them in their hearts (Jer. 31:33–34).

Verses 17–18 says, "And their sins and iniquities will I remember no more. Now where remission of these is, there is no more offering for sin."

Hebrews 10:19–22, The Day of Atonement

The only time the high priest could enter into the Holy of Holies was on the Day of Atonement. It was also the time for cleansing the temple. Verses 19–20 says, "Having therefore, brethren, boldness to enter into the holiest by the blood of Jesus, By a new and living way, which he hath consecrated for us, through the veil, that is to say, his flesh."

When Christ was crucified and died on the cross, the veil in the temple tore from the top down (Matt. 27:51; Mark 15:38), symbolizing Christ making access for us. Having received the holy spirit, we are now spiritually holy so we can enter into the throne room of God.

Verse 21 says, "And having an high priest over the house of God." The word "high" is the figure of speech heterosis of degree, meaning "highest priest." Jesus Christ is the high priest after the order of Melchizedek.

Verse 22 says, "Let us draw near with a true heart in full assurance of faith, having our hearts sprinkled from an evil conscience, and our bodies washed with pure water." This phrase, "let us draw near," is used in the book of Hebrews in the sacrificial and priestly sense. The sprinkling of blood and washing of water symbolized cleansing and purification.

In Leviticus 16, the whole chapter is referring to the Day of Atonement. In verse 4, Aaron is instructed to wash in water. Then in verse 14, he sprinkles the blood from the sacrifice on the mercy seat of the ark. Finally in verses 18–19, he takes some of the blood and sprinkles on the horns of the altar seven times to cleanse it and consecrate it from the uncleanness of the children of Israel. Our sprinkling is Christ's shed blood for us, and our washing is the holy spirit. (See 1 Peter 1:2 and Titus 3:5–6.)

Hebrews 10:23–25, Feast of Tabernacles

This final section in Hebrews, with respect to the feast days, deals with our blessed hope. Verse 23 says, "Let us hold fast the profession of our faith without wavering; (for He is faithful that promised) [1 Cor. 1:9, 10:13]."

This word for "faith" is really the word "hope." It is the Greek word *elpis*. The root word *elpo* means "to anticipate." Remember that in the Feast of Tabernacles, the whole feast pointed toward the hope by using imagery of tents and booths that were temporary dwelling places.

Verses 24–25 says, "And let us consider one another to provoke unto love and to good works: Not forsaking the assembling of ourselves together, as the manner of some is; but exhorting one another: [should desire to be with] and so much more, as we see the day approaching." This phrase "let us consider one another" is beautifully translated in the Aramaic translation, "And we should **gaze** on one another."[33]

Just as the Last Great Day of the Feast of Tabernacles pointed to the hope, we look toward that day approaching when Christ will come back for us and we shall reign with Him on high.

---

[33] Magiera, *Aramaic Peshitta New Testament Translation*, 525.

Appendix 2
The Trump of God

I would like to refer to a most important verse written to the church regarding the trump of God. First Thessalonians 4:16 says, "For the Lord himself shall descend from heaven with a shout, with the voice of the archangel, and with the trump of God: and the dead in Christ shall rise first."

We saw in chapter 9 that the Feast of Trumpets, or Tishri 1, was Israel's marking of the new year and that God also marked it out as a high holy day (Num. 29:1; Lev. 23:23–25).

On the Day of Atonement in the Year of Jubilee was a special event for blowing the trumpets. Leviticus 25:8–10 says,

> And thou shalt number seven Sabbaths of years unto thee, seven times seven years; and the space of the seven Sabbaths of years shall be unto thee forty and nine years. Then shalt thou cause the trumpet of the jubilee to sound on the tenth day of the seventh month, in the day of atonement shall ye make the trumpet sound throughout all your land. And ye shall hallow the fiftieth year, and proclaim liberty throughout all the land unto all the inhabitants thereof: it shall be a jubilee unto you; and ye shall return every man unto his possession, and ye shall return every man unto his family.

As Israel experienced the trump of God on Mount Sinai, so we will one day experience the trump of God when Christ returns for us. Exodus 19:13–19 says,

> There shall not an hand touch it, but he shall surely be stoned, or shot through; whether it be beast or man, it shall not live: when the trumpet soundeth long, they shall come up to the mount. And Moses went down from the mount unto the people, and sanctified the people; and they washed their clothes. And he said unto the people, Be ready against the third day: come not at your wives. And it came to pass on the third day in the morning, that there were thunders and lightnings, and a thick cloud upon the mount, and the voice of the trumpet exceeding loud; so that all the people that was in the camp trembled. And Moses brought forth the people out of the camp to meet with God; and they stood at the nether part of the mount. And mount Sinai was altogether on a smoke, because the LORD descended upon it in fire: and the smoke thereof ascended as the smoke of a furnace, and the whole mount quaked

greatly. And when the voice of the trumpet sounded long, and waxed louder and louder, Moses spake, and God answered him by a voice.

Israel witnessed this. Can you picture this event? God speaking directly to all of Israel? Wow! Exodus 20:18 says, "And all the people saw the thunderings, and the lightnings, and the noise of the trumpet, and the mountain smoking: and when the people saw it, they removed, and stood afar off."

It says in the next verse that they did not want God to speak directly with them. Exodus 20:19 says, "And they said unto Moses, Speak thou with us, and we will hear: but let not God speak with us, lest we die."

God told Moses to make two silver trumpets for specific purposes. This is recorded in Numbers. Numbers 10:1–10 says,

> And the LORD spake unto Moses, saying, Make thee two trumpets of silver; of a whole piece shalt thou make them: that thou mayest use them for the calling of the assembly, and for the journeying of the camps. And when they shall blow with them, all the assembly shall assemble themselves to thee at the door of the tabernacle of the congregation. And if they blow but with one trumpet, then the princes, which are heads of the thousands of Israel, shall gather themselves unto thee. When ye blow an alarm, then the camps that lie on the east parts shall go forward. When ye blow an alarm the second time, then the camps that lie on the south side shall take their journey: they shall blow an alarm for their journeys. But when the congregation is to be gathered together, ye shall blow, but ye shall not sound an alarm. And the sons of Aaron, the priests, shall blow with the trumpets; and they shall be to you for an ordinance for ever throughout your generations. And if ye go to war in your land against the enemy that oppresseth you, then ye shall blow an alarm with the trumpets; and ye shall be remembered before the LORD

your God, and ye shall be saved from your enemies. Also in the day of your gladness, and in your solemn days, and in the beginnings of your months, ye shall blow with the trumpets over your burnt offerings, and over the sacrifices of your peace offerings; that they may be to you for a memorial before your God: I am the LORD your God. Israel was to blow these trumpets at the sighting of the new moon, which marked the beginning of each month, and at the beginning of all of the feast days. It was to be a memorial before God.

There were three types of trumpets Israel used: the *shopar* (*shofar* or ram's horn), the *hasosra* (a three-foot-long, slender, silver trumpet also known as the *chatsotserah*), and the *qeren* (a cornet used in Babylon).

The *shopar* is used seventy-two times. The word is related to Akkadian *shapparu*, "wild sheep," and Arabic *sawafirun*, "ram's horns." In the Old Testament, it is always used of the curved musical instrument made of the horn of a ram. The general word for the horn of an animal is *qeren*.[34]

The *chatsotserah*, "trumpet," was a long, straight, and slender wind instrument, such as Moses was commanded to furnish for the service of the Israelites. Josephus gives this description, "In length it was little less than a cubit. It was composed of a narrow tube, somewhat thicker than a flute, but with so much breadth as was sufficient for admission of the breath of a man's mouth; it ended in the form of a bell, like common trumpets." – Antiquities, book III, chap. 12 § 6.[35]

When David brought back the ark, he had them blow the trumpets. Second Samuel 6:12–15 reads,

And it was told king David, saying, The LORD hath blessed the house of Obededom, and all that pertaineth unto him, because of the ark of God. So David went and brought up the ark of God from the house of Obededom into the city of David with gladness. And it was so,

---

[34] Harris, *Theological Wordbook of the Old Testament*, 951.
[35] Freeman, *Manners and Customs of the Bible*, 229.

that when they that bare the ark of the Lord had gone six paces, he sacrificed oxen and fatlings. And David danced before the Lord with all his might; and David was girded with a linen ephod. So David and all the house of Israel brought up the ark of the Lord with shouting, and with the sound of the trumpet.

When Solomon was coroneted as king, they blew the trumpets. First Kings 1:34, 39 reads,

And let Zadok the priest and Nathan the prophet anoint him there king over Israel: and blow ye with the trumpet, and say, God save king Solomon … And Zadok the priest took an horn of oil out of the tabernacle, and anointed Solomon. And they blew the trumpet; and all the people said, God save king Solomon.

Trumpets were also used for praise. Psalm 81:1–3 says, "Sing aloud unto God our strength: make a joyful noise unto the God of Jacob. Take a psalm, and bring hither the timbrel, the pleasant harp with the psaltery. Blow up the trumpet in the new moon, in the time appointed, on our solemn feast day."

Psalm 150:3 reads, "Praise him with the sound of the trumpet: praise him with the psaltery and harp." And 2 Chronicles 5:13 states,

It came even to pass, as the trumpeters and singers were as one, to make one sound to be heard in praising and thanking the Lord; and when they lifted up their voice with the trumpets and cymbals and instruments of musick, and praised the Lord, saying, For he is good; for his mercy endureth for ever: that then the house was filled with a cloud, even the house of the Lord.

These trumpets were also used to gather the children of Israel. Isaiah 27:12–13 says,

> And it shall come to pass in that day, that the LORD shall beat off from the channel of the river unto the stream of Egypt, and ye shall be gathered one by one, O ye children of Israel. And it shall come to pass in that day, that the great trumpet shall be blown, and they shall come which were ready to perish in the land of Assyria, and the outcasts in the land of Egypt, and shall worship the LORD in the holy mount at Jerusalem.

There is no surprise that it says in 1 Thessalonians 4:16 that God will use a trumpet for the gathering together of the church.

Jeremiah 6:1, 16–18 reads,

> O ye children of Benjamin, gather yourselves to flee out of the midst of Jerusalem, and blow the trumpet in Tekoa, and set up a sign of fire in Bethhaccerem: for evil appeareth out of the north, and great destruction … Thus saith the LORD, Stand ye in the ways, and see, and ask for the old paths, where is the good way, and walk therein, and ye shall find rest for your souls. But they said, We will not walk therein. Also I set watchmen over you, saying, Hearken to the sound of the trumpet. But they said, We will not hearken. Therefore hear, ye nations, and know, O congregation, what is among them.

The blowing of trumpets was also used to warn God's people. Ezekiel 6 talks about the watchmen. Ezekiel 33:1–6 says,

> Again the word of the Lord came unto me, saying, Son of man, speak to the children of thy people, and say unto them, When I bring the sword upon a land, if the people of the land take a man of their coasts, and set him for their watchman: If when he seeth the sword come upon the land, he blow the trumpet, and warn the people; Then whosoever heareth the sound of the trumpet, and taketh not warning; if the sword come, and take him

away, his blood shall be upon his own head. He heard the sound of the trumpet, and took not warning; his blood shall be upon him. But he that taketh warning shall deliver his soul. But if the watchman see the sword come, and blow not the trumpet, and the people be not warned; if the sword come, and take any person from among them, he is taken away in his iniquity; but his blood will I require at the watchman's hand.

The blowing of trumpets is connected with the "day of the Lord" or the "last day." Joel 2:1 says, "Blow ye the trumpet in Zion, and sound an alarm in my holy mountain: let all the inhabitants of the land tremble: for the day of the LORD cometh, for it is nigh at hand."

Jesus tells the apostles about the end times. Matthew 24:29–31 reads,

Immediately after the tribulation of those days shall the sun be darkened, and the moon shall not give her light, and the stars shall fall from heaven, and the powers of the heavens shall be shaken: And then shall appear the sign of the Son of man in heaven: and then shall all the tribes of the earth mourn, and they shall see the Son of man coming in the clouds of heaven with power and great glory. And he shall send his angels with a great sound of a trumpet, and they shall gather together his elect from the four winds, from one end of heaven to the other.

It was also used to call a sacred assembly. Joel 2:15 says, "Blow the trumpet in Zion, sanctify a fast, call a solemn assembly."

War was another reason they blew the trumpets. God is going to blow the trumpet and fight for Israel. Zechariah 9:14–17 states,

And the LORD shall be seen over them, and his arrow shall go forth as the lightning: and the LORD God shall blow the trumpet, and shall go with whirlwinds of the south. The LORD of hosts shall defend them; and they shall devour, and subdue with sling stones; and they shall drink, and make a noise as through wine; and they shall be filled like bowls, and as the corners of the altar. And the LORD their God shall save them in that day as the flock of his people: for they shall be as the stones of a crown, lifted up as an ensign upon his land. For how great is his goodness, and how great is his beauty! corn shall make the young men cheerful, and new wine the maids.

Second Chronicles 13:14–15 reads,

And when Judah looked back, behold, the battle was before and behind: and they cried unto the LORD, and the priests sounded with the trumpets. Then the men of Judah gave a shout: and as the men of Judah shouted, it came to pass, that God smote Jeroboam and all Israel before Abijah and Judah.

In the book of Revelation, a trumpet is also used metaphorically as the voice of God or an angel. Revelation 1:10 says, "I was in the Spirit on the Lord's day, and heard behind me a great voice, as of a trumpet." And Revelation 4:1 states, "After this I looked, and, behold, a door was opened in heaven: and the first voice which I heard was as it were of a trumpet talking with me; which said, Come up hither, and I will shew thee things which must be hereafter."

It also says that there were seven angels who stood before God, who were given seven trumpets. Revelation 8:1–2 says, "And when he had opened the seventh seal, there was silence in heaven about the space of half an hour. And I saw the seven angels which stood before God; and to them were given seven trumpets."

We looked at how these trumpets were used throughout the Word of God. For the church, we look forward to that great day when God will gather together the one body with the shout of an archangel and the trump of God. 1 Corinthians 15:52 says, "In a moment, in the twinkling of an eye, at the last trump: for **the trumpet shall sound**, and the dead shall be raised incorruptible, and we shall be changed."

Appendix 3
Abide in Christ

John 14–15 reveals God's desire to dwell in us and we in Him. John 14:2 says, "In my Father's house are many mansions: if it were not so, I would have told you. I go to prepare a **place for you**." And verse 10 speaks, "Believest thou not that I am in the Father, and the Father in me? the words that I speak unto you I speak not of myself: but the Father that **dwelleth in me**, he doeth the works."

Verses 16–17 says,

> And I will pray the Father, and he shall give you another Comforter, that he may **abide with you** for ever; Even the Spirit of truth; whom the world cannot receive, because it seeth him not, neither knoweth him: but ye know him; for **he dwelleth with you**, and **shall be in you.**

Verse 23 reads, "Jesus answered and said unto him, If a man love me, he will keep my words: and my Father will love him, and **we will come unto him**, and **make our abode with him."** And verse 25 says, "These things have I spoken unto you, being yet present with you."

Jesus declared that the spirit of truth dwelled **with** them but foretold that the spirit would be **in** them. On that day, they would know that He and the Father would make their abode with them. That day came on the Feast of Pentecost.

The word "abide" in verse 16 is the Greek word *meno* and is translated "abide, abode, dwell, remain, and mansions." It is used seventeen times in John 14–15 and is used forty-two times in the Gospel as a whole.

This making their abode in us exists in a very personal way. We are to have a deep, intimate relationship with God the Father and with His Son, Jesus Christ. It is by way of His spirit dwelling in us that allows us to have this personal relationship. Jesus Christ came to reveal the Father. We cannot know God apart from Jesus Christ.

Philippians 3:10 says, "That I may know him, and the power of his resurrection, and the fellowship of his sufferings, being made conformable unto his death."

The Amplified Bible, Classic Edition (AMPC) translates this verse the following way,

> [For my determined purpose is] that I may know Him [that I may progressively become more deeply and intimately acquainted with Him, perceiving and recognizing and understanding the wonders of His Person more strongly and more clearly], and that I may in that same way come to know the power outflowing from His resurrection [which it exerts over believers], and that I may so share His sufferings as to be continually transformed [in spirit into His likeness even] to His death.

In *Experiencing God: Knowing and Doing the Will of God*, the authors write the following,

> We are an industrious people. We always want to accomplish something. The idea of doing God's will sounds exciting. Once in a while someone says, "Don't just stand there—do something." Sometimes individuals or churches are so busy carrying out plans they think will help achieve God's purposes that they don't bother to find out what he actually wants. We often wear ourselves out and accomplish little for the kingdom of God.
>
> I think God is crying out to us: "Don't just do something. Stand there! Enter into a love relationship with Me. Get to know Me. Adjust your life to Me. Let Me love you and teach you about Myself as I work

through you." A time will come when action is required, but we must not short-circuit the relationship (Ps. 37:7). Your relationship with God must come first. Out of your walk with God, He accomplishes His plans for our world.

Jesus said, "I am the vine; you are the branches. The one who remains in Me and I in him produces much fruit, because you can do nothing without Me." (John 15:5). Do you believe that without Him you can do nothing? Sure, you can keep yourself busy. You can immerse yourself in activities, programs, meetings, and events, but they will not have lasting value for God's kingdom. The apostle Paul warned that one day every person's work would be tested by fire to see if it was done according to God's will and divine power (1 Cor. 3:13). The activities God will command in the final judgement will be those which He initiated. If you are experiencing a time of spiritual dryness in your life, you may be trying to do things on your own that God has not initiated. However, when you abide in Christ, you will be amazed at what God accomplishes through your life.

God wants you to gain a greater knowledge of Him my experience. That's what abiding in Him will do for you. He wants a love relationship with you, and He wants to involve you in His kingdom work. He alone can initiate His plans. He wants your involvement, but you cannot do it for Him. When you believe Him and do as He directs, then He will accomplish His work through you.[36]

A Tabernacle, A Temporary Dwelling Place

A tabernacle was a temporary dwelling place. Even the temple was not God's ultimate dwelling place. Acts 7:44–50 says,

---

[36] Henry Blackaby, Richard Blackaby, and Claude King, *Experiencing God: Knowing and Doing the Will of God* (Nashville: B & H Publishing, 2003), 33–34.

> Our fathers had the tabernacle of witness in the wilderness, as he had appointed, speaking unto Moses, that he should make it according to the fashion that he had seen. Which also our fathers that came after brought in with Jesus [Joshua] into the possession of the Gentiles, whom God drave out before the face of our fathers, unto the days of David; Who found favour before God, and desired to find a tabernacle for the God of Jacob. But Solomon built him an house. Howbeit the most High dwelleth not in temples made with hands; as saith the prophet, Heaven is my throne, and earth is my footstool: what house will ye build me? saith the Lord: or what is the place of my rest? Hath not my hand made all these things?

God dwells not in temples made with hands. Now God dwells in us by way of His spirit in us. Romans 8:9 says, "But ye are not in the flesh, but in the Spirit, if so be that the Spirit of God dwell in you. Now if any man have not the Spirit of Christ, he is none of his."

Our bodies are considered a temple for the spirit to dwell in. This is the figure of speech metaphor meaning one thing represents another. 1 Corinthians. 6:19–20 reads,

> What? know ye not that your body is the temple of the Holy Ghost which is in you, which ye have of God, and ye are not your own? For ye are bought with a price: therefore glorify God in your body, and in your spirit, which are God's.

We have this spirit in the earthen vessels. 2 Corinthians 4:6–7 states,

> For God, who commanded the light to shine out of darkness, hath shined in our hearts, to give the light of the knowledge of the glory of God in the face of Jesus Christ. But we have this treasure in earthen vessels,

that the excellency of the power may be of God, and not of us.

We are clothed with the holy spirit. We will get the heavenly body when Christ comes back (1 Cor. 15:44–58). 2 Corinthians 5:1–3 reads,

> For we know that if our earthly house of this tabernacle were dissolved, we have a building of God, an house not made with hands, eternal in the heavens. For in this we groan, earnestly desiring to be clothed upon with our house which is from heaven: If so be that being clothed we shall not be found naked.

Here the blessed hope of resurrection is described as being clothed upon with the heavenly body. This is the subject that commences at 2 Corinthians 4:14. In 2 Corinthians 5:3, the *kai* is ignored in both A.V. and R.V. The Greek is, "if indeed BEING CLOTHED also, we shall not be found naked [*as some among you say*]." There are some amoung the Corinthians who said "there is no resurrection of the dead" (1 Cor. 15:12, 35), and here those assertions are thus referred to.[37]

The "if indeed being clothed" emphasizes that we will not be found naked. 2 Corinthians 5:4–5 reads,

> For we that are in this tabernacle do groan, being burdened: not for that we would be unclothed, but clothed upon, that mortality might be swallowed up of life. Now he that hath wrought us for the selfsame thing is God, who also hath given unto us the earnest of the Spirit.

Verses 6–8 says,

> Therefore we are always confident, knowing that, whilst we are at home in the body, we are absent from the Lord:

---

[37] Bullinger, *Figures of Speech Used in the Bible*, 51.

(For we walk by faith, not by sight:) We are confident, I say, and willing rather to be absent from the body, and to be present with the Lord. Wherefore we labour, that, whether present or absent, we may be accepted of him. For we must all appear before the judgment seat of Christ; that every one may receive the things done in his body, according to that he hath done, whether it be good or bad.

E. W. Bullinger in *Figures of Speech Used in the Bible* writes the following regarding verses 6–8,

> Here the change is from participles to finite verbs: "Being confident then always, and conscious that being at home [here] in the body, we are from home, away from the Lord (for by faith we are walking, not by sight). We are confident, however, and are content rather to be from home [here] out of the body, and to be at home with the Lord [there]."
>
> These words are usually misquoted "absent from the body, present with the Lord," as though it meant that the moment we are absent from the body we are present with the Lord. But this is exactly what is does not say; and the [figure of speech] *Anacoluthon* call our attention to this.
>
> The whole subject is resurrection, starting from 4:14. Our new bodies are contrasted in v. 1-5: vis.: "the earthly house of this tabernacle (i.e., this mortal body)" is contrasted with "our (*oikeeteerion*), our *spiritual* or resurrection body" (see Jude 6): vis.: "our house which is from heaven," the future body of glory being called "house," as compared with the present body in which we groan, which is called a "tabernacle" or tent.
>
> The argument is that, while we are in this "tabernacle" we cannot have that "house"; and that while we are in the tent we are away from our real eternal home, which

is with the Lord. There is no thought (here or elsewhere) of our being at home, or "with the Lord," apart from resurrection and our resurrection bodies.

The figure of speech Anacoluthon is "A breaking off the sequence of thought." - An´-a-co-lu´-thon, from *a* or *av, negative,* and (*akolouthos*), following: i.e., *not following,* want of sequence or connection in a sentence, the latter part of which does not follow on or correspond with the former part.

This figure is so-called, because the construction with which a proposition begins is abandoned; and, either for the sake of perspicuity, emphasis, or elegance, the sentence proceeds in a manner, different from that in which it set out.

Human writings of deep thought or feeling or argument frequently have the figure *Anacoluthon,* which in these cases is mere irregularity attributable to inadvertence, arising from the negligence or carelessness of the writer.[38]

In the King James Version, this section of 2 Corinthians is choppy, but if you read it from the Greek or Aramaic, one will see the flow of the context.

We have a living hope. Hope is not static. First Peter 1:3 says, "Blessed be the God and Father of our Lord Jesus Christ, which according to his abundant mercy hath begotten us again unto a lively hope by the resurrection of Jesus Christ from the dead."

Building the Building

Another metaphor used is that we are a building collectively. Ephesians 2:6 says, "And hath raised us up together, and made us sit together in heavenly places in Christ Jesus: [From God's perspective this is already done]."

---

[38] Ibid., 720–722.

Ephesians 2:20–22 reads,

> And are **built** upon the foundation of the apostles and prophets, Jesus Christ himself being the chief corner stone; In whom all the building **fitly framed** together groweth unto an holy temple in the Lord: In whom ye also are **builded** together for an habitation of God through the Spirit.

We are built upon a solid foundation that has been already laid for us. As lively stones, we are also part of this building (1 Peter 2:4).

The word "fitly framed" is the Greek word *sunarmologeomai* and is a combination of three Greek words: *sun*, a preposition meaning "with or together;" *armo* from the root meaning "chariot" (as ancient chariot makers were carpenters); and *logeomai*, the basic meaning "to speak." The combination of these words literally means "to join" (a carpentry term) or "to glue together or fit" together with the words spoken by Jesus Christ, the apostles, and prophets.

The word "builded" is the Greek word *oikodomee*, meaning "the work itself," that is, in progress. This Greek word comes from two words. *Oikia* means "house, a physical building," and *doma* comes from the word "demo," "to build," literally meaning "to build a house."

Ephesians 3:17 says, "That Christ may dwell [same root word as *oikodomee*] in your hearts by faith; that ye, being rooted and grounded in love." And Ephesians 4:16 reads, "From whom the whole body fitly joined together and compacted by that which every joint supplieth, according to the effectual working in the measure of every part, maketh increase of the body unto the edifying of itself in love."

First Peter 2:5 states, "Ye also, as lively stones, are built up a spiritual house, an holy priesthood, to offer up spiritual sacrifices, acceptable to God by Jesus Christ." For the context, read verses 1–9.

In Hebrews, it is the promise of hope of our faith. Hebrews 10:23–25 says,

> Let us hold fast the profession of our faith without wavering; (for he is faithful that promised;) And let

us consider one another to provoke unto love and to good works: Not forsaking the assembling of ourselves together, as the manner of some is; but exhorting one another: and so much the more, as ye see the day approaching.

This phrase "assembling of ourselves together" is the same word translated "the gathering together" in 2 Thessalonians 2:1. We are to stir one another up in love and good works, as we are abiding in Christ, knowing that one day we will dwell with Him permanently. And we are to exhort one another as we wait for Christ to come back.

Colossians 3:4 says, "When Christ, who is our life, shall appear, then shall ye also appear with him in glory."

Until this day comes, we are to abide in Him and He in us.

Appendix 4
Rejoice Before the Lord

It is God's desire and will that we rejoice before Him for all He has blessed us with and made. It is amazing that some Christians think of their walk with God as one without pleasures or enjoyment. But I want to show from God's Word that this is the farthest thing from the truth.

Deuteronomy 26:11 says, "And thou shalt rejoice in every good thing which the Lord thy God hath given unto thee, and unto thine house, thou, and the Levite, and the stranger that is among you." And Deuteronomy 27:7 says, "And thou shalt offer peace offerings, and shalt eat there, and rejoice before the Lord thy God."

Every feast day and at every free will offering, God wanted His people to rejoice before Him. Deuteronomy 12:5–8 states,

> But unto the place which the Lord your God shall choose out of all your tribes to put his name there, even unto his habitation shall ye seek, and thither thou shalt come: And thither ye shall bring your burnt offerings, and your sacrifices, and your tithes, and heave offerings of your hand, and your vows, and your freewill offerings, and the firstlings of your herds and of your flocks: And there ye shall eat before the Lord your God, and ye shall rejoice in all that ye put your hand unto, ye and your households, wherein the Lord thy God hath blessed thee. Ye shall not do after all the things that we do here this day, every man whatsoever is right in his own eyes.

In the context, God tells them to destroy all idol worship in the lands they are going to possess. Then it clearly states in verse 8 that they were not to do what they think is right, but what He commanded them. Deuteronomy 14:22–23 says,

> Thou shalt truly tithe all the increase of thy seed, that the field bringeth forth year by year. And thou shalt eat before the LORD thy God, in the place which he shall choose to place his name there, the tithe of thy corn, of thy wine, and of thine oil, and the firstlings of thy herds and of thy flocks; that thou mayest learn to fear the LORD thy God always.

God said He would choose the place and they may learn to reverence him. Verses 24–25 reads,

> And if the way be too long for thee, so that thou art not able to carry it; or if the place be too far from thee, which the LORD thy God shall choose to set his name there, when the LORD thy God hath blessed thee: [This tithe was from what God had blessed them with.] Then shalt thou turn it into money, and bind up the money in thine hand, and shalt go unto the place which the LORD thy God shall choose:

Have you ever prayed about where you should give the firstfruits of what God had blessed you with? Read on and you will gain some insight into areas that God considered important. Verses 26–29 says,

> And thou shalt bestow that money for whatsoever thy soul lusteth after, for oxen, or for sheep, or for wine, or for strong drink, or for whatsoever thy soul desireth: and thou shalt eat there before the LORD thy God, and thou shalt rejoice, thou, and thine household, And the Levite that is within thy gates; thou shalt not forsake him; for he hath no part nor inheritance with thee. At the end

of three years thou shalt bring forth all the tithe of thine increase the same year, and shalt lay it up within thy gates: And the Levite, (because he hath no part nor inheritance with thee,) and the stranger, and the fatherless, and the widow, which are within thy gates, shall come, and shall eat and be satisfied; that the LORD thy God may bless thee in all the work of thine hand which thou doest.

Israel was to remember their deliverance from the enslavement in Egypt. God wants us to enjoy what He has made for us and blessed us. Deuteronomy 16:11–14 says,

And thou shalt rejoice before the LORD thy God, thou, and thy son, and thy daughter, and thy manservant, and thy maidservant, and the Levite that is within thy gates, and the stranger, and the fatherless, and the widow, that are among you, in the place which the LORD thy God hath chosen to place his name there. And thou shalt remember that thou wast a bondman in Egypt: and thou shalt observe and do these statutes. Thou shalt observe the feast of tabernacles seven days, after that thou hast gathered in thy corn and thy wine: And thou shalt rejoice in thy feast, thou, and thy son, and thy daughter, and thy manservant, and thy maidservant, and the Levite, the stranger, and the fatherless, and the widow, that are within thy gates.

The word for "rejoice" in these verses is the Hebrew word *samach*. The first usage of this word *samach* is used in Exodus 4, where it sets the tone of how this word is used as far as gladness is concerned. Exodus 4:14 reads,

And the anger of the LORD was kindled against Moses, and he said, Is not Aaron the Levite thy brother? I know that he can speak well. And also, behold, he cometh

> forth to meet thee: and when he seeth thee, he will be
> **glad [*samach*] in his heart.**

This word *samach* is translated to "rejoice, be glad, joyful, merry, merrily and merry hearted." It is usually translated as "rejoice or be glad." Leviticus 23:40 says, "And ye shall take you on the first day the boughs of goodly trees, branches of palm trees, and the boughs of thick trees, and willows of the brook; and ye shall rejoice before the LORD your God seven days. [Feast of Tabernacles]."

The root *samach* denotes being glad and joyful, with the whole disposition as indicated by its association of the heart, soul, and the lightening up of the eyes. The Lord and His salvation are cited most frequently as the reason for joy. Indeed the joy of the Lord is man's strength, and many verses call upon man to share this joy. Thus Israel is called upon to rejoice at its festivals and central sanctuary.[39]

In Zephaniah is a beautiful display of God's tenderness and love. Zephaniah 3:17 reads, "The LORD thy God in the midst of thee is mighty; he will save, he will rejoice over thee with joy; he will rest in his love, he will joy over thee with singing."

It is God's will that we rejoice (1 Thess. 5:16–18). In the Old Testament times, they rejoiced because of what God had blessed them with. He really wanted them to have a great time, especially at the feasts. He wanted them to have a joyous time. Today we are to rejoice in what God has done for us through Jesus Christ. When we come together in a fellowship, we are to rejoice with each other as well as before God. In our personal lives, He desires for us to have loving and intimate relationships with Him.

God made Israel rejoice with great joy. Ezra 6:22 says, "And they kept the Feast of Unleavened Bread seven days with joy; for the LORD made them joyful, and turned the heart of the king of Assyria toward them, to strengthen their hands in the work of the house of God, the God of Israel."

Nehemiah 12:43 reads, "Also that day they offered great sacrifices, and rejoiced, for God had made them rejoice with great joy; the women

---

[39] Harris, *Theological Wordbook of the Old Testament, Vol. 2*, 879.

and the children also rejoiced, so that the joy of Jerusalem was heard afar off."

We have seen that, in the times of the Old Testament, God marked out many yearly feasts and it was a time of great rejoicing. These feasts pointed toward the coming one and what He would accomplish (salvation). Jesus has brought us into an intimate fellowship with our heavenly Father. Today we can have a continual feast and rejoice in what God has accomplished for us through Jesus Christ.

Joy in the Hope

It is interesting to note that the theme of Thessalonians is the hope, and we are exhorted to rejoice in this hope. First Thessalonians 1:6 says, "And ye became followers of us, and of the Lord, having received the word in much affliction, with joy of the Holy Ghost."

First Thessalonians 2:19–20 reads, "For what is our hope, or joy, or crown of rejoicing? Are not even ye in the presence of our Lord Jesus Christ at his coming?" And 1 Thessalonians 3:9 states, "For what thanks can we render to God again for you, for all the joy wherewith we joy for your sakes before our God."

We are to rejoice for the sake of each other before our God. Our rejoicing is in the hope.

Romans 5:2, 11 says, "By whom also we have access by faith into this grace wherein we stand, and rejoice in hope of the glory of God ... And not only so, but we also joy in God through our Lord Jesus Christ, by whom we have now received the atonement."

Romans 12:12 reads, "Rejoicing in hope; patient in tribulation; continuing instant in prayer." And 2 Corinthians 1:12–14 states,

> For our rejoicing is this, the testimony of our conscience, that in simplicity and godly sincerity, not with fleshly wisdom, but by the grace of God, we have had our conversation in the world, and more abundantly to you-ward. For we write none other things unto you, than what ye read or acknowledge; and I trust ye shall acknowledge even to the end; As also ye have acknowledged us in

part, that we are your rejoicing, even as ye also are ours in the day of the Lord Jesus.

Hebrews 3:6 says, "But Christ as a son over his own house; whose house are we, if we hold fast the confidence and the rejoicing of the hope firm unto the end."

This is our confidence to rejoice while looking forward to Christ's return.

First Peter 1:6–8 reads,

Wherein ye greatly rejoice, though now for a season, if need be, ye are in heaviness through manifold temptations: That the trial of your faith, being much more precious than of gold that perisheth, though it be tried with fire, might be found unto praise and honour and glory at the appearing of Jesus Christ: Whom having not seen, ye love; in whom, though now ye see *him* not, yet believing, ye **rejoice** with **joy** unspeakable and full of glory: Our joy is full and our joy and rejoicing continues, because of the hope we have of looking forward to Christ's return.

Joy and Boasting

This word for "rejoice and joy" is also used in the verb sense in the fashion "to boast and glory." Romans 15:15–17 says,

Nevertheless, brethren, I have written the more boldly unto you in some sort, as putting you in mind, because of the grace that is given to me of God, That I should be the minister of Jesus Christ to the Gentiles, ministering the gospel of God, that the offering up of the Gentiles might be acceptable, being sanctified by the Holy Ghost. I have therefore whereof I may glory through Jesus Christ in those things which pertain to God.

This word for "glory" in verse 17 is the word to "boast, to rejoice." We rejoice through Jesus Christ in the things that pertain to God. True boasting, glorying, and rejoicing always magnifies God and pertains to Him. To get a sense of how these words are used together, let's look at Romans 5.

Romans 5:1–2 says, "Therefore being justified by faith, we have peace with God through our Lord Jesus Christ: By whom also we have access by faith into this grace wherein we stand, and **rejoice** in hope of the glory of God."

We have access by faith, and we can stand in God's presence and rejoice in the hope of the glory of God because we know that Christ is coming back one day to gather us up. We can also rejoice now because it's Christ in you the hope of glory.

Verses 3–5 states,

> And not only so, but we **glory** in tribulations also: knowing that tribulation worketh patience; And patience, experience; and experience, hope: And hope maketh not ashamed; because the love of God is shed abroad in our hearts by the Holy Ghost which is given unto us.

The word "rejoice" in verse 2 and the word "glory" in verse 3 are the same Greek word. The reason why we can glory in tribulation is because of verse 2, where it says we can "rejoice in the hope of the glory of God."

Joy and Rejoicing with One Another

The keywords in Philippians are "joy" and "rejoicing." Philippians 2:16–18 says,

> Holding forth the word of life; that I may rejoice in the day of Christ, that I have not run in vain, neither laboured in vain. Yea, and if I be offered upon the sacrifice and service of your faith, I joy, and rejoice with

you all. For the same cause also do ye joy, and rejoice with me.

We are also to rejoice in the service and sacrifice of helping one another's faith. Philippians 3:1, 3 says,

> Finally, my brethren, rejoice in the Lord. To write the same things to you, to me indeed is not grievous, but for you it is safe ... For we are the circumcision, which worship God in the spirit, and rejoice in Christ Jesus, and have no confidence in the flesh.

Philippians 4:4 reads, "Rejoice in the Lord always: and again I say, Rejoice." This is in a command form. We can be inwardly joyful even when things seem dreary. Christ set the example. Hebrews 12:2–3 states,

> Looking unto Jesus the author and finisher of our faith; who **for the joy that was set before him** endured the cross, despising the shame, and is set down at the right hand of the throne of God. For consider him that endured such contradiction of sinners against himself, lest ye be wearied and faint in your minds.

The J. B. Phillips New Testament translation renders this "because of the joy he knew would follow his suffering." It is a hard thing to imagine that Christ knew the sufferings He would have to endure, yet He saw past it toward the glory that would follow, thus having the presence of joy.

We have seen that, in the Old Testament, God's will was for Israel to rejoice before Him. Now of everything that we are to do, we are to rejoice. The occasion for joy is manifold and is always with God. God wants us to rejoice in the present because our hope is a lively hope. According to God, it is done.

First Peter 4:13 says, "But rejoice, inasmuch as ye are partakers of Christ's sufferings; that, when his glory shall be revealed, ye may be glad also with exceeding joy."

Appendix 5
Luke 9:51–53

I want to take a closer look at these verses in Luke 9. Luke 9:51 says, "And it came to pass, when the time was come that he should be received up, he stedfastly set his face to go to Jerusalem."

It was time to go to Jerusalem for the Feast of Tabernacles. (All males were required to attend.) And it is possible that He could have gone to the other two feasts preceding it (Tishri 1, the Blowing of the Trumpets and the Day of Atonement), which occurred ten days later, although those two feasts were not mandatory for all males to attend.

Verses 52–53 says, "And sent messengers before his face: and they went, and entered into a village of the Samaritans, to make ready for him. And they did not receive him, because his face was as though he would go to Jerusalem."

Most commentaries and explanations regarding these verses say that Jesus Christ was referring to His ascension even though it was about seven to eight months in the future. The Greek word used here for "received up" is *analepsis*, meaning "to ascend." This is the only occurrence of this word in the New Testament and is used here as a noun. The verb form is the Greek word *analambano* and is used thirteen times in the New Testament, four times in reference to Christ's ascension.

However, this is one of the records that is not explained by the Greek but rather because of the Hebraism behind it. There are many records that say when people were going to Jerusalem that they would "go up" or "went up." Why? Because it was on top of a mountain. People today use the same words when going up in elevation or going north.

Psalms 120–134 are called "Songs of Ascents." They were sung as people walked up toward Jerusalem for the feast days.

John Gills' *Exposition of the Entire Bible* has the following explanation,

> And it came to pass, when the time was come, … Or "days were fulfilled", an usual Hebraism; when the period of time fixed for his being in Galilee was come to an end: when he had fulfilled his ministry, and finished all his sayings, and wrought all the miracles he was to work in those parts; when he was to quit this country, and go into Judea, and up to Jerusalem, signified in the next clause: that he should be received up; or as all the Oriental versions rightly render the words, "when the time, or days of his ascension were fulfilled"; not of his ascension to heaven, as interpreters generally understand the passage, because the word is used of that, in much less as others, of his being taken and lifted up from the earth upon the cross, and so signifies his crucifixion, and sufferings, and death; for of neither of these can it be said, that the time of them was come, or the days fulfilled, in which either of these should be: for if Christ was now going to the feast of tabernacles, as some think, it must be above half a year before his death, and still longer before his ascension to heaven: and if to the feast of dedication, it was above three months to his ascension: hence interpreters that go this way, are obliged to interpret it, that the time drew near, or was drawing on, or the days were almost fulfilled; whereas the expression is full and strong, that the time was come, and the days were fulfilled; and which was true in the sense hinted at, that now the time was up, that Jesus must leave the low lands of Galilee, having finished his work there; and go into the higher country of Judea, and so up to Jerusalem; for of

his ascension from Galilee to Jerusalem are the words to be understood.[40]

Not only was Jesus Christ determined to go to the Feast of Tabernacles, He was purposed in going to the Judea area for the rest of His earthly ministry. Jesus coming to Samaria was on route to Jerusalem from Galilee in the north. The reason this is important to understand is because it relates to a timeline of events that occurred and where Jesus Christ travelled and when.

Map of Christ's travels: Galilee, Samaria, Jericho, and finally Jerusalem

---

[40] John Gill, *John Gill's Exposition on the Entire Bible*, www.christianity.com/bible/commentary.php?com=gill&b=42&c=9.

John 6:4

I would like to clear up a misunderstood verse that explains the timeline of the events in John 6–7. Not understanding John 6:4 is why many believe that Jesus Christ's ministry lasted three years instead of one year of their holy calendar and seventy weeks of the civil calendar. In John, it states it was Passover, but there are two reason that this feast mentioned here is not Passover.

We are told they were by the Sea of Galilee, but Jesus and every other adult male made the Jerusalem pilgrimage at the feasts of Passover, Pentecost, and Tabernacles. For this feast to be Passover would mean that Jesus and a huge assembly of obedient worshippers decided to defy God by staying in Tiberias, which is impossible for the sinless Lamb of God. What is equally unlikely is the mass defiance of the requirement to eat only unleavened bread at this time. The bread referred to in this passage is the Greek word Strong's 740, *artos*, "leavened bread." Unleavened bread is the Greek word Strong's 106, *azumos*.

So to consider John 6:4 as a Passover, we have to accept a verse not found in the earliest manuscripts; believe that the Messiah and His otherwise obedient followers defied God by not going to Jerusalem for the feast; and recognize they further defied God by eating a type of bread that was forbidden during this time.

It is far more likely that this verse represents a nonpilgrimage feast when leavened bread was eaten. Although no text confirms this, the whole of the word must be employed to the understanding of this verse.[41]

---

41 Ibid.

Appendix 6
The Branch

There are five accounts in the Old Testament of the word "branch," which deals with the coming Messiah. The word "branch" is in uppercase (BRANCH) in the King James Version in Zechariah and the "B" is in upper case in Jeremiah. Each one of the records that mentions "the branch" points to an attribute of the Messiah and correlates to a specific gospel that highlights these attributes. It was covered in chapter 9 on the significance of Tishri 1 and that Jesus Christ was born on Tishri 1.

Jeremiah 23:5 says, "Behold, the days come, saith the Lord, that I will raise unto David a righteous Branch, and a **King** shall reign and prosper, and shall execute judgment and justice in the earth."

This verse says that the righteous "branch" will be a **king**. In Jeremiah, it also states that he would be a king.

Jeremiah 33:14–15 says,

> Behold, the days come, saith the Lord, that I will perform that good thing which I have promised unto the house of Israel and to the house of Judah. In those days, and at that time, will I cause the Branch of righteousness to **grow up unto David**; and he shall execute judgment and righteousness in the land.

He was to be a king after the lineage of King David. The gospel that this correlates to is Matthew. The book of Matthew starts out with the royal lineage from David to Christ. Matthew 2:2 is the record of the wise men seeking a king, and verse six records the prophesy from Micah

5:2, "a Governor, that shall rule my people Israel." In Matthew 27:37 at Christ's crucifixion, it was written, "this is Jesus the King of the Jews." Then Matthew ends with, "All power is given unto me in heaven and in earth" (Matt. 28:18).

Zechariah also mentions this word, "branch." Zechariah 3:8 says, "Hear now, O Joshua the high priest, thou, and thy fellows that sit before thee: for they are men wondered at: for, behold, I will bring forth my **servant** the BRANCH."

This account states that the "branch" would be a **servant**. The gospel that this correlates to is Mark. Mark records no genealogy, as a servant does not gain his position by descent. Mark begins with Jesus Christ's ministry. The word translated "lord" or "sir" is the Greek word *kurios*. It is used seventy-three times of Jesus Christ in the other three gospels but only three times in Mark, for a servant is not called a lord. Mark puts great stress on Jesus's actions in the service of God to His fellowman. Thus, the gospel of Mark emphasizes Jesus Christ as a servant willing to accept responsibility in serving and helping others."[42]

Zechariah 6:12 says, "And speak unto him, saying, Thus speaketh the LORD of hosts, saying, Behold the **man** whose name is The BRANCH; and he shall grow up out of his place, and he shall build the temple of the LORD."

This record indicates that the "branch" would be a **man**. And the gospel this correlates to is Luke. Luke 3:23–38 traces Jesus's genealogy from the beginning of man, Adam, and comes down to Joseph, Jesus's stepfather.

Let's look at the final record in Isaiah. Isaiah 4:2 says, "In that day shall the **branch of the LORD** be beautiful and glorious, and the fruit of the earth shall be excellent and comely for them that are escaped of Israel."

This is the only record where "branch" is in the lowercase in the King James Version. But the word "branch" used in all five of these records is the Hebrew word *semah*, which means simply "sprout or shoot." In this record, the "branch" is the **offspring of the Lord**. He came as

---

[42] Wierwille, *Jesus Christ Our Passover*, 449.

God's Son. The gospel this correlates to is John. The gospel of John states Christ was the only begotten in John 1:14, 18, 34.

The word for "branch" (*semah*) is used thirty-two times in the Old Testament. Its general meaning conveyed is "growing, building, and sprouting." Each of these five records is all related to the coming up of a shoot from the root or seed of David.

Second Samuel 23:5 says, "Although my house be not so with God; yet he hath made with me an everlasting covenant, ordered in all things, and sure: for this is all my salvation, and all my desire, although he make it not to grow [sprout]." And Psalm 132:17 states, "There will I make the horn of David to bud [sprout]: I have ordained a lamp for mine anointed."

It will spring forth for the whole house of Israel.

Ezekiel 29:21 reads, "In that day will I cause the horn of the house of Israel to bud forth [sprout], and I will give thee the opening of the mouth in the midst of them; and they shall know that I am the Lord."

Using the Septuagint to translate *semah* from Hebrew to Greek, we find two references in the New Testament (Luke 1:78; Heb. 7:14). The Greek words are *anatole* and *anatello*, "our Lord sprang forth."

Hebrews 7:14 says, "For it is evident that our Lord sprang out of Juda; of which tribe Moses spake nothing concerning priesthood." And Luke 1:78 reads, "Through the tender mercy of our God; whereby the dayspring from on high hath visited us."

There is a very incredible link between the written Word of God and the word written in the stars. A woman is in reference to the constellation of Virgo. Virgo, as the initial sign of the zodiac, indicates her headship of the other eleven signs of the zodiac.[43] This record presents essential information on the exact time of Christ's birth.

Revelation 12:1–5 says,

> And there appeared a great wonder in heaven; a woman clothed with the sun, and the moon under her feet, and upon her head a crown of twelve stars: And she being with child cried, travailing in birth, and pained to be delivered. And there appeared another wonder in

---

[43] E. W. Bullinger, *Witness of the Stars*, 20–22.

heaven; and behold a great red dragon, having seven heads and ten horns, and seven crowns upon his heads. And his tail drew the third part of the stars of heaven, and did cast them to the earth: and the dragon stood before the woman which was ready to be delivered, for to devour her child as soon as it was born. And she brought forth a man child, who was to rule all nations with a rod of iron: and her child was caught up unto God, and to his throne.

In this sign, there is a star of the first magnitude in her left hand. (See the illustration on page 129.) This star is an Arabic word called *Al Zimach*. This is the same word in Hebrew, *El Tsemech*. It is of no coincidence that this constellation represents the beginning of the cycle of the zodiac. Tishri 1 represents the beginning of the civil calendar. The birth of Christ was at the exact time the sun and moon, the celestial equator, in this constellation. The elliptic of the sun at sunset and the moon appearing on the horizon marked the first day of Tishri. Some people believe the sphinx in Egypt is a symbol of the beginning and ending of the Zodiac cycle. Virgo is the head of the women, the head of the year. Leo is the tail, or end of the year.

In Arabic, this sign is called "branch." In Latin, the word "virgin" came from *Virga*, meaning "branch."

We have seen that this word for "branch" in the Old Testament means sprout, in reference to the coming Messiah, who would be of seed of David. This was also foretold of the promised seed in Genesis 3:15, which was corroborated in Revelation 12:1.

Genesis 3:15 says, "And I will put enmity between thee and the woman, and between thy seed and her seed; it shall bruise thy head, and thou shalt bruise his heel."

We saw the attributes of this righteous branch in connection with the four gospels. But I want to look closer at the first two records in Jeremiah that seem to be pointing to the gospel of Matthew. As we read these verses, I want to emphasize the differences and suggest there could be another gospel that Jeremiah 23:5 is referring to.

Constellation of Virgo with the branch in her left hand

Jeremiah 23:5 says, "Behold, the days come, saith the LORD, that I will raise unto David a righteous Branch, and a King shall **reign** and prosper, and shall execute judgment and justice in the earth."

The key words that make this different from Jeremiah 33:14–15 are "a King shall reign." In Jeremiah 33:14–15, there is no mention of a king reigning.

When Jesus Christ came, He did execute judgment and displayed righteousness throughout the land. When He entered Jerusalem the second time on the day called the Triumphal Entry, that is when He executed judgment. And when He walked about, He ministered throughout the land with righteousness. But He did not reign. When will that happen? This points to another gospel, the book of Revelation, because that is where it says that the King will come back and reign (the millennial reign). That is when this verse in Jeremiah 23:5 will be fulfilled.

Appendix 7
Chronological Timeline of the Feasts during the Times of Jesus Christ

Occasion with Feast Days	Date		Year	Scripture Reference
	Judean Calendar	Modern Calendar		
Passover	Nisan 14	April 9 Sunset	27 AD	John 2:13 John 4:45
Feast of Unleavened Bread	Nisan 15-22	April 10-18 Sunset	27 AD	John 2:23*
* The Feast of Passover is translated "Unleavened Bread" in Aramaic.				
Feast of Weeks Pentecost	Sivan 7	May 31 Sunset	27 AD	John 5:1-47
Tishri 1 Blowing of Trumpets	Tishri 1	September 20 Sunset	27 AD	John 6:4* John 6:15**
* See Appendix 5. ** Tishri 1 was the day kings were anointed.				
Day of Atonement	Tishri 10	September 30 Sunset	27 AD	Matthew 15:1* Mark 7:1*
* Context: The oral traditions of the Pharisees could point to this feast day. This was the day of cleansing of the Temple. Later it was a national day of fasting.				
Feast of Tabernacles	Tishri 15-21	October 4-11 Sunset	27 AD	John 7:1-53*
* Feast of Tabernacles ended and everyone went home.				
Feast of Dedication	Chislev 25	November - December	27 AD	John 10:22-35*
2nd Passover	Nisan 12-17	April 26 - May 1	28 AD	Matthew 26:14-ff Mark 14:10-ff Luke 22:3-ff John 13:1-ff

Appendix 8
The Feast of Dedication

The following is an excerpt from *The Acceptable Day of the Lord* by Walter J. Cummins regarding the Feast of Dedication,

> It was not a feast of Mosaic law, but rather it originated during the time of the Maccabees in the second century BC, long after Malachi was written. The former records in the Scriptures preceding the Gospel records relate what occurred after the Judeans had returned from their captivity in the land of Babylon and when they were being ruled by the Persians. However, in the second century BC, the Judeans were no longer ruled by the Persians but rather by the Seleucids, and during that time, the Judeans revolted because the Seleucids had desecrated the Temple at Jerusalem. After the Judeans gained their independence, they cleansed and dedicated the Temple in December of 164 BC. This dedication became a yearly feast at Jerusalem celebrated for eight days beginning on the twenty-fifth day of the ninth month, which was Kislev. Since the Judean months were determined by the appearance of the new moon, Kislev could have had either 29 or 30 days, and the eight day of the Feast of Dedication could have occurred on either the second or the third day of the tenth month, which was Tebeth. This feast had no bearing on the law.[44]

---

[44] Cummins, *The Acceptable Year of the Lord*, 57–58.

Although this was not a feast day of the Lord, Jesus Christ did attend this feast, knowing there was an opportunity to minister to those who were in attendance. John 10:22–39 says,

> And it was at Jerusalem the feast of the dedication, and it was winter. And Jesus walked in the temple in Solomon's porch. Then came the Jews round about him, and said unto him, How long dost thou make us to doubt? If thou be the Christ, tell us plainly. Jesus answered them, I told you, and ye believed not: the works that I do in my Father's name, they bear witness of me. But ye believe not, because ye are not of my sheep, as I said unto you. My sheep hear my voice, and I know them, and they follow me: And I give unto them eternal life; and they shall never perish, neither shall any man pluck them out of my hand. My Father, which gave them me, is greater than all; and no man is able to pluck them out of my Father's hand. I and my Father are one. Then the Jews took up stones again to stone him. Jesus answered them, Many good works have I shewed you from my Father; for which of those works do ye stone me? The Jews answered him, saying, For a good work we stone thee not; but for blasphemy; and because that thou, being a man, makest thyself God. Jesus answered them, Is it not written in your law, I said, Ye are gods? If he called them gods, unto whom the word of God came, and the scripture cannot be broken; Say ye of him, whom the Father hath sanctified, and sent into the world, Thou blasphemest; because I said, I am the Son of God? If I do not the works of my Father, believe me not. But if I do, though ye believe not me, believe the works: that ye may know, and believe, that the Father is in me, and I in him. Therefore they sought again to take him: but he escaped out of their hand.

Christ may have linked Himself to this feast in two ways. First was the cleansing of the temple, after Judas Maccabaeus drove out Antiochus

Epiphanes when he defiled the temple. And next is when Christ was being sanctified by God in John 10:36. The feast was also called the Feast of Lights. Jesus Christ revealed Himself as the light of the world in John 9:5.

The other feast called Purim was on Adar 13–16, when the book of Esther was read. There is no reference to this feast in the New Testament.

Appendix 9
The Day of the Lord

The phrase "the day of the Lord" is used many times throughout the Bible. It is used to point to a time when God will come to restore His people Israel. It is also used of a time when the Messiah will come back and reign in Jerusalem in the millennial. And it is used of a time when Christ will come back for His saints in the Christian church.

Isaiah 2:12 says, "For the **day of the Lord** of hosts shall be upon every one that is proud and lofty, and upon every one that is lifted up; and he shall be brought low."

Similar expressions were used, for example, "in that day," which can refer to ordinary, expected events as well as the end times. The Lord's day is not the weekly Sabbath or Sunday in our culture. But the Lord's day is His day on Earth, when the Lord Himself shall rule in righteousness, power, and glory.

The Day of the Lord in the Old Testament

"The day of the Lord" first appears in Isaiah 2:12. Verse 11 says, "The lofty looks of man shall be humbled, and the haughtiness of men shall be bowed down, and the Lord alone shall be exalted in that day." The phrase "in that day" is used numerous times in the prophetic writings.

Isaiah 2:2 says, "And it shall come to pass **in the last days**, that the mountain of the Lord's house shall be established in the top of the mountains, and shall be exalted above the hills; and all nations shall flow unto it."

Isaiah 2:2 sets the time of this phrase, "in the last days." The whole book of Obadiah refers to God's judgement on Edom, and the key words used are "day" and "day of the Lord." Obadiah is a snapshot of all the prophetic writings. Old Testaments prophets used the phrase "day of the Lord" to mark, in Israel's history, when God would judge all nations that came against Israel. God will restore Israel, but Israel will first have to lament and repent.

Amos 5:1–4 [Lamentation] says,

> Hear ye this word which I take up against you, even a lamentation, O house of Israel. The virgin of Israel is fallen; she shall no more rise: she is forsaken upon her land; there is none to raise her up. For thus saith the Lord God; The city that went out by a thousand shall leave an hundred, and that which went forth by an hundred shall leave ten, to the house of Israel. For thus saith the Lord unto the house of Israel, Seek ye me, and ye shall live.

Amos 5:5–15 [Repentence] reads,

> But seek not Bethel, nor enter into Gilgal, and pass not to Beersheba: for Gilgal shall surely go into captivity, and Bethel shall come to nought. Seek the Lord, and ye shall live; lest he break out like fire in the house of Joseph, and devour it, and there be none to quench it in Bethel. Ye who turn judgment to wormwood, and leave off righteousness in the earth, Seek him that maketh the seven stars and Orion, and turneth the shadow of death into the morning, and maketh the day dark with night: that calleth for the waters of the sea, and poureth them out upon the face of the earth: The Lord is his name: That strengtheneth the spoiled against the strong, so that the spoiled shall come against the fortress. They hate him that rebuketh in the gate, and they abhor him that speaketh uprightly. Forasmuch therefore as your treading is upon the poor, and ye take from him

burdens of wheat: ye have built houses of hewn stone, but ye shall not dwell in them; ye have planted pleasant vineyards, but ye shall not drink wine of them. For I know your manifold transgressions and your mighty sins: they afflict the just, they take a bribe, and they turn aside the poor in the gate from their right. Therefore the prudent shall keep silence in that time; for it is an evil time. Seek good, and not evil, that ye may live: and so the Lord, the God of hosts, shall be with you, as ye have spoken. Hate the evil, and love the good, and establish judgment in the gate: it may be that the Lord God of hosts will be gracious unto the remnant of Joseph.

Amos 9:11–15 [Restoration] states,

For, lo, I will command, and I will sift the house of Israel among all nations, like as corn is sifted in a sieve, yet shall not the least grain fall upon the earth. All the sinners of my people shall die by the sword, which say, The evil shall not overtake nor prevent us. In that day will I raise up the tabernacle of David that is fallen, and close up the breaches thereof; and I will raise up his ruins, and I will build it as in the days of old: That they may possess the remnant of Edom, and of all the heathen, which are called by my name, saith the Lord that doeth this. Behold, the days come, saith the Lord, that the plowman shall overtake the reaper, and the treader of grapes him that soweth seed; and the mountains shall drop sweet wine, and all the hills shall melt. And I will bring again the captivity of my people of Israel, and they shall build the waste cities, and inhabit them; and they shall plant vineyards, and drink the wine thereof; they shall also make gardens, and eat the fruit of them. And I will plant them upon their land, and they shall no more be pulled up out of their land which I have given them, saith the Lord thy God.

Joel also states that destruction will first come. Joel 1:15 says, "Alas for the day! for the day of the Lord is at hand, and as a destruction from the Almighty shall it come."

In Joel 2, it states that "the day of the Lord" is coming. Joel 2:1 reads, "Blow ye the trumpet in Zion, and sound an alarm in my holy mountain: let all the inhabitants of the land tremble: for the day of the Lord cometh, for it is nigh at hand."

Then verse 12 is a call to repentance, "Therefore also now, saith the Lord, turn ye even to me with all your heart, and with fasting, and with weeping, and with mourning."

In Joel 3, it says that God will bring back all captives of Judah and Jerusalem. He will gather all nations and judge them, and He will bless His people. Joel 3:14, 18 says,

> Multitudes, multitudes in the valley of decision: for the day of the Lord is near in the valley of decision ... And it shall come to pass in that day, that the mountains shall drop down new wine, and the hills shall flow with milk, and all the rivers of Judah shall flow with waters, and a fountain shall come forth out of the house of the Lord, and shall water the valley of Shittim.

In Zephaniah is the great day of the Lord. Zephaniah 1:7–18 reads,

> Hold thy peace at the presence of the Lord God: for the day of the Lord is at hand: for the Lord hath prepared a sacrifice, he hath bid his guests. And it shall come to pass in the day of the Lord's sacrifice, that I will punish the princes, and the king's children, and all such as are clothed with strange apparel. In the same day also will I punish all those that leap on the threshold, which fill their masters' houses with violence and deceit. And it shall come to pass in that day, saith the Lord, that there shall be the noise of a cry from the fish gate, and an howling from the second, and a great crashing from the hills. Howl, ye inhabitants of Maktesh, for all the

merchant people are cut down; all they that bear silver are cut off. And it shall come to pass at that time, that I will search Jerusalem with candles, and punish the men that are settled on their lees: that say in their heart, The Lord will not do good, neither will he do evil. Therefore their goods shall become a booty, and their houses a desolation: they shall also build houses, but not inhabit them; and they shall plant vineyards, but not drink the wine thereof. **The great day of the Lord** is near, it is near, and hasteth greatly, even the voice of the day of the Lord: the mighty man shall cry there bitterly. That day is a day of wrath, a day of trouble and distress, a day of wasteness and desolation, a day of darkness and gloominess, a day of clouds and thick darkness, A day of the trumpet and alarm against the fenced cities, and against the high towers. And I will bring distress upon men, that they shall walk like blind men, because they have sinned against the Lord: and their blood shall be poured out as dust, and their flesh as the dung. Neither their silver nor their gold shall be able to deliver them in the day of the Lord's wrath; but the whole land shall be devoured by the fire of his jealousy: for he shall make even a speedy riddance of all them that dwell in the land.

In Zephaniah 2 is the call for repentance and judgement of the nations. Then at the end of this book (Zephaniah 3:14) come the blessings. Zephaniah 3:14–20 says,

> Sing, O daughter of Zion; shout, O Israel; be glad and rejoice with all the heart, O daughter of Jerusalem. The Lord hath taken away thy judgments, he hath cast out thine enemy: the king of Israel, even the Lord, is in the midst of thee: thou shalt not see evil any more. In that day it shall be said to Jerusalem, Fear thou not: and to Zion, Let not thine hands be slack. The Lord thy God in the midst of thee is mighty; he will save, he will rejoice

over thee with joy; he will rest in his love, he will joy over thee with singing. I will gather them that are sorrowful for the solemn assembly, who are of thee, to whom the reproach of it was a burden. Behold, at that time I will undo all that afflict thee: and I will save her that halteth, and gather her that was driven out; and I will get them praise and fame in every land where they have been put to shame. At that time will I bring you again, even in the time that I gather you: for I will make you a name and a praise among all people of the earth, when I turn back your captivity before your eyes, saith the Lord.

Do you see this pattern? Almost all of the prophetic books are like this.

God shows Zechariah many visions, including the prophesy of "the branch," the coming Messiah. He promises Israel that He will dwell in the midst of Jerusalem, "Thus saith the Lord; I am returned unto Zion, and will dwell in the midst of Jerusalem (Zech. 8:3a). In Zechariah 9 is the promise of the coming king.

Zechariah 9:9 states, "Rejoice greatly, O daughter of Zion; shout, O daughter of Jerusalem: behold, thy King cometh unto thee: he is just, and having salvation; lowly, and riding upon an ass, and upon a colt the foal of an ass."

In Zechariah 10, we see the restoration of Judah and Israel. Then in Zechariah 14 is the "day of the Lord." In this prophesy, the Messiah returns to the Mount of Olives. Zechariah 14:1–4 says,

Behold, the day of the Lord cometh, and thy spoil shall be divided in the midst of thee. For I will gather all nations against Jerusalem to battle; and the city shall be taken, and the houses rifled, and the women ravished; and half of the city shall go forth into captivity, and the residue of the people shall not be cut off from the city. Then shall the Lord go forth, and fight against those nations, as when he fought in the day of battle. And his feet shall stand in that day upon the mount of Olives, which is before Jerusalem on the east, and the mount of Olives shall cleave in the midst thereof toward the east and toward the west, and there shall be a very great valley; and half of the mountain shall remove toward the north, and half of it toward the south.

In verse 9, it states the Lord will be king, "And the Lord shall be king over all the earth: in that day shall there be one Lord, and his name one." This is the beginning of the millennial reign. All nations will come and worship this king at the Feast of Tabernacles.

Zechariah 14:16 says, "And it shall come to pass, that every one that is left of all the nations which came against Jerusalem shall even go up from year to year to worship the King, the Lord of hosts, and to keep the feast of tabernacles."

Micah also speaks of this day. Micah 4:1, 6 says, "But in the last days it shall come to pass, that the mountain of the house of the Lord shall be established in the top of the mountains, and it shall be exalted above the hills; and people shall flow unto it … In that day, saith the Lord, will I assemble her that halteth, and I will gather her that is driven out, and her that I have afflicted."

We close this section on the day of the Lord in the Old Testament with the book of Malachi and the promise of the coming Messiah. Malachi 4:5 says, "Behold, I will send you Elijah the prophet before the coming of the great and dreadful day of the Lord."

The Day of the Lord in the Gospels

These prophesies of the coming Messiah came to pass when Christ was born in Bethlehem, the righteous branch, Immanuel. When Jesus Christ spoke of "this day" or "the day of the Lord," it was always in the context of the kingdom of Heaven. It is first mentioned in Matthew.

Matthew 7:21–22 says,

Not every one that saith unto me, Lord, Lord, shall enter into the kingdom of heaven; but he that doeth the will of my Father which is in heaven. Many will say to me

> in that day, Lord, Lord, have we not prophesied in thy
> name? and in thy name have cast out devils? and in thy
> name done many wonderful works?

Jesus mentions "the day of Judgement" four times in the Gospels. Matthew 10:15 says, "Verily I say unto you, It shall be more tolerable for the land of Sodom and Gomorrha in the day of judgment, than for that city." Matthew 11:22, 24 reads, "But I say unto you, It shall be more tolerable for Tyre and Sidon at the day of judgment, than for you ... But I say unto you, That it shall be more tolerable for the land of Sodom in the day of judgment, than for thee."

Matthew 12:36 states, "But I say unto you, That every idle word that men shall speak, they shall give account thereof in the day of judgment." And Mark 6:11 says, "And whosoever shall not receive you, nor hear you, when ye depart thence, shake off the dust under your feet for a testimony against them. Verily I say unto you, It shall be more tolerable for Sodom and Gomorrha in the day of judgment, than for that city."

Jesus is sitting with His disciples on the Mount of Olives, and they ask Him about His second coming and the end times. Matthew 24:3 says, "And as he sat upon the mount of Olives, the disciples came unto him privately, saying, Tell us, when shall these things be? and what shall be the sign of thy coming, and of the end of the world?"

He then warns them to not be deceived and said they should be not troubled. He promises that those who will endure to the end will be saved. They will go through tribulations. Some will be killed. But the gospel of the kingdom has to reach nations before the end will come. In verse 15, He tells them the prophesy of Daniel has to come to pass.

The Pharisees ask Jesus when the kingdom of God will come. Luke 17:20 says, "And when he was demanded of the Pharisees, when the kingdom of God should come, he answered them and said, The kingdom of God cometh not with observation."

He quickly points out that it will not be with observation, and He also compares it to Noah and Lot's days of its sudden coming. We must be expecting and always looking for his coming.

Luke 21 is a parallel record of Matthew 24, except that Luke adds in "the coming of the Son of man." In verses 25–28, he mentions there will be signs in the heavens, distress of nations, and sea and waves roaring. "And then shall they will see the Son of man coming in a cloud with power and great glory."

The Transition

I want to consider a difference between Jesus Christ as the Messiah to Israel and Jesus Christ as our Lord and Savior. I also want to show the contrast between the bride of Israel and the church, the one body. To Israel, He is the bridegroom to the bride, the promised Messiah. In the future, He will be their king after David's lineage. When He comes back to earth, He will reign as king to Israel.

To the church, Jesus Christ is our Savior and the head of the body of Christ. He is our brother. We are joint heirs with Christ. It is Christ in us. When He gathers us up, we will be with Him and our Father forever.

Acts 1 is the transitional period between the time of Israel and the church administration. Israel's time is on hold until the fullness of the Gentiles is come in (Rom. 11:25). Then the events in Daniel and the book of Revelation unfold.

According to Acts 1:9, the apostles watched Jesus ascend up into the clouds, and two men (angels) who stood by them asked, "Which also said, Ye men of Galilee, why stand ye gazing up into heaven? This same Jesus, which is taken up from you into heaven, shall so come in like manner as ye have seen him go into heaven." They were standing on the Mount of Olives. When He comes back, it will be at the Mount of Olives. This will fulfill the prophesy in Zechariah. But remember, Jesus Christ also said they would see the Son of Man coming in the clouds with power and glory.

Zechariah 14:4 says,

> And his feet shall stand in that day upon the mount of Olives, which is before Jerusalem on the east, and the mount of Olives shall cleave in the midst thereof toward the east and toward the west, and there shall be a very great valley; and half of the mountain shall remove toward the north, and half of it toward the south.

Israel saw a day prophesied about God pouring out His blessings on the Gentiles, but did not know of the great mystery that was revealed to Paul. Isaiah 11:10 says, "And in that day there shall be a root of Jesse, which shall stand for an ensign of the people; to it shall the Gentiles seek: and his rest shall be glorious."

The Day of the Lord and the Church Today

This great mystery was that the Jews and Gentiles would be of the same body. Ephesians 2:16, 3:6 says, "And that he might reconcile both unto God in one body by the cross, having slain the enmity thereby … That the Gentiles should be fellowheirs, and of the same body, and partakers of his promise in Christ by the gospel." And 1 Corinthians 15:20 reads, "But now is Christ risen from the dead, and become the firstfruits of them that slept."

Christ is the firstfruits of those fallen asleep. We in the church age (who are alive at His coming) will be given a new body. There is no mention of that for the bride of Israel. It was not a mystery that all would die and be in one of the resurrections.

John 5:29 says, "And shall come forth; they that have done good, unto the resurrection of life; and they that have done evil, unto the resurrection of damnation." And Daniel 12:2 states, "And many of them that sleep in the dust of the earth shall awake, some to everlasting life, and some to shame and everlasting contempt."

The mystery pertained to the church. In Thessalonians, it says some will be alive and some will be asleep when He returns. This will happen in a moment, a nanosecond, and the trumpet shall sound. First Thessalonians 1:10 says, "And to wait for his Son from heaven, whom he raised from the dead, even Jesus, which delivered us from the wrath to come."

We are instructed to wait for Christ to come back. This is our hope. We are delivered from the wrath to come. It doesn't say we are spared from trials, tribulations, and temptations, but from wrath. Why? Because contrary to Israel, we are promised that we are saved from the wrath to come. By believing in Jesus Christ, we have already been judged. We have been justified, sanctified, and made righteous.

Romans 4:25 says, "Who was delivered for our offences, and was raised again for our justification." 2 Corinthians 5:21 reads, "For he hath made him to be sin for us, who knew no sin; that we might be made the righteousness of God in him."

This "day of the Lord" will also come as a thief in the night, as mentioned in Thessalonians 5:2. Let's look at the comforting words Paul gives us in the previous chapter.

First Thessalonians 4:13–18 says,

> But I would not have you to be ignorant, brethren, concerning them which are asleep, that ye sorrow not, even as others which have no hope. For if we believe that Jesus died and rose again, even so them also which sleep in Jesus will God bring with him. For this we say unto you by the word of the Lord, that we which are alive and remain unto the coming of the Lord shall not prevent them which are asleep. For the Lord himself shall descend from heaven with a shout, with the voice of the archangel, and with the trump of God: and the dead in Christ shall rise first: Then we which are alive and remain shall be caught up together with them in the clouds, to meet the Lord in the air: and so shall we ever be with the Lord. Wherefore comfort one another with these words.

"The Lord will descend from heaven with a shout." This word "shout" means "a call, summons, or a shout that assembles."[45] Then it says there will be "the voice of an archangel" (*phonee*) and the trump of God "at the last trump." Paul continues in chapter 5 to tell comforting words.

In 1 Thessalonians 5:1, Paul says there is no need for him to write about the time and seasons. Why? Because we know that the day of the Lord so comes as a thief in the night. In verse 5, he says, "Ye are all the children of light, and the children of the day." He encourages us

---

[45] Walter J. Cummins, *A Journey through the Acts and Epistles* (Franklin: Scripture Consulting, 2006), 487.

that we are not of the darkness, but rather children of the day. This is a Hebraism and a metaphor, which gives a quality and characteristic to the subject. We are light.

Ephesians 5:8 says, "For ye were sometimes darkness, but now are ye light in the Lord: walk as children of light."

We are light, children of light. We are not going to be in the dark about the coming of the Lord. As children of the day, we are to be watchful, sober, loving, and remaining steadfast in our hope.

Paul also reiterates that God has not appointed us to wrath. What a comfort to know this. Knowing this, Paul continues to tell them not to be troubled or shaken as "the day of Christ (should be Lord) is at hand."

Second Thessalonians 2:1–3 reads,

> Now we beseech you, brethren, by the coming of our Lord Jesus Christ, and by our gathering together unto him, That ye be not soon shaken in mind, or be troubled, neither by spirit, nor by word, nor by letter as from us, as that the day of Christ is at hand. Let no man deceive you by any means: for that day shall not come, except there come a falling away first, and that man of sin be revealed, the son of perdition;

Verse 3 is referring to the day of the Lord and that it should not come, except there comes a falling away first. In time sequence, this falling away must come before the day of the Lord. The gathering together will come prior to both of these events. See Daniel 12 regarding the prophesy about the day of the Lord and the lawless one.

Walter J. Cummins in *A Journey through the Acts and Epistles* notes the following,

> The word "falling away" is the Greek word *apostasia* meaning departure. The cognate neuter noun *apostasion* occurs three times (Matthew 5:31, 19:7, Mark 10:4) of "divorce," the departure of a husband and wife from each other. The word used here is a feminine noun with only one other occurrence in the New Testament, namely, in

Acts 21:21 regarding "departure" from Moses, that is, a departure from the Mosaic law. The departure referred to here is explained in verses 6-8 as the removal of a restraint. Verse 1 began this discussion with regard to the coming of the Lord Jesus Christ and our gathering up together to him. This passage in chapter 2 taken together with the previous verses in the first suggests that the "departure" refers to the gathering together of the holy ones, which precedes both the appearance of the lawless one and the day of the Lord.[46]

Second Thessalonians 2:4–8 reads,

Who opposeth and exalteth himself above all that is called God, or that is worshipped; so that he as God sitteth in the temple of God, shewing himself that he is God. Remember ye not, that, when I was yet with you, I told you these things? And now ye know what withholdeth that he might be revealed in his time. For the mystery of iniquity doth already work: only he who now letteth will let, until he be taken out of the way. And then shall that Wicked be revealed, whom the Lord shall consume with the spirit of his mouth, and shall destroy with the brightness of his coming.

In verse 5, it says "remember ye not." The question is introduced in Greek with the Greek negative adverb *ou*, which is used in questions to anticipate an affirmative answer, "yes." In verse 6, it says, "and ye know what withholdeth." This refers to what restrains the son of destruction from being revealed in the present time and is explained in verse 7 as something that must be taken out of the way before He can be revealed in His own time. For this reason, the departures mentioned in verse 3 refer to the departure of this restraint, after which the lawless one will be

---

[46] Ibid., 487.

revealed. God, our heavenly Father, is certainly the One who restrains until He determines to remove the restraint. [47]

It also mentions the brightness of the lawless one. The word "brightness" is the Greek word *epiphaneia*, meaning "appearance or shining forth." Here it is used to refer to the appearance of the coming of the man of lawlessness, whose coming is according to the working of Satan, as stated in verse 9.[48] Remember Satan was called the angel of light (2 Cor. 11:14). "And no marvel; for Satan himself is transformed into an angel of light." We are the children of the day. God, our heavenly Father, is certainly the One who restrains.

- "I am the light of the world, he that followeth me shall not walk in darkness, but shall have the light of life" (John 8:12).
- "The day is at hand … and let us put on the armor of light … let us walk honestly, as in the day" (Rom. 13:12–13).
- "That ye may be blameless in the day of our Lord Jesus Christ" (1 Cor. 1:8).
- "In the day of the Lord we will be each other's rejoicing" (2 Cor. 1:14).
- "We have this perfect work being performed until the day of Jesus Christ and that we may approved things excellent and be sincere and without offence until the day of Christ" (Phil. 1:6, 10).
- "We are persuaded and committed unto him against that day" (2 Tim. 1:12).
- "A crown of righteousness awaits us in that day" (2 Tim. 4:8).

We have seen how the day of the Lord was used in the Old Testament and the prophets' foretelling of the coming Messiah. They did not, however, understand that the suffering of Christ must first happen before they would see His glory to follow. We also saw how Jesus Christ spoke of Himself and the day still to come of judgement.

Luke 4:18–19 says,

---

[47] Ibid., 488.
[48] Ibid., 489.

The Spirit of the Lord is upon me, because he hath anointed me to preach the gospel to the poor; he hath sent me to heal the brokenhearted, to preach deliverance to the captives, and recovering of sight to the blind, to set at liberty them that are bruised, To preach the acceptable year of the Lord.

This is a quote from Isaiah 61. He read half of verse 2, "to preach the acceptable year of the Lord," and then stopped and did not read the rest of the verses from Isaiah. This is what His first coming was to accomplish and fulfill. Isaiah 61:2b continues, "and the day of vengeance of our God; to comfort all that morn." This is still in the future, to be fulfilled.

Hebrews 8:8 says, "For finding fault with them, he saith, Behold, the days come, saith the Lord, when I will make a new covenant with the house of Israel and with the house of Judah." And 1 Thessalonians 5:8–9 reads, "But let us, who are of the day, be sober, putting on the breastplate of faith and love; and for an helmet, the hope of salvation. For God hath not appointed us to wrath, but to obtain salvation by our Lord Jesus Christ."

And one day, in His time, He will send Christ back to gather us together, to meet Him in the air. And so shall we ever be with the Lord.

Bibliography

Bergey, David. *Jesus Christ Our Approach Offering.* 2004

Berry, George Ricker. *The Interlinear Literal Translation of the Greek New Testament.* 1958. Reprint, Grand Rapids: Zondervan, 1979

Blackaby, Henry, Richard Blackaby, and Claude King. *Experiencing God: Knowing and Doing the Will of God.* Nashville: B & H Publishing Group, 2008.

Bullinger, E. W. *Figures of Speech Used in the Bible.* 1893. Reprint, Grand Rapids: Baker Book House, 1968.

———. *How to Enjoy the Bible.* 1907. Reprint, New Knoxville: American Christian Press, 1983.

———. *The Companion Bible.* 1964. Reprint, Grand Rapids: Zondervan, 1974.

———. *The Witness of the Stars.* 1893. Reprint, Grand Rapids: Kregel, 1967.

Cummins, Walter J. *A Journey through the Acts and Epistles.* Franklin: Scripture Consulting, 2006.

———. *The Acceptable Year of the Lord.* 2nd ed. Franklin: Scripture Consulting, 2005.

Douglas, J. D. *The New Bible Dictionary.* 1962. Reprint, Grand Rapids: Wm. B. Eerdmans, 1962.

Edersheim, Alfred. *Sketches of Jewish Social Life.* 1987. Reprint, Grand Rapids: Wm. B. Eerdmans.

———. *The Life and Times of Jesus the Messiah.* 2016. Rev. ed. (complete and unabridged in one volume), Grand Rapids: Hendrickson, 1993.

Fausset, A. R. *Bible Cyclopaedia Critical and Expository.* Hartford: The S. S. Scranton Company, 1911.

Finegan, Jack. *Handbook of Biblical Chronology*. 1998. Rev. ed., Peabody: Hendrickson, 1964.

Freeman, James M. *Manners and Customs of the Bible*. 1972. Reprint, New York: Logos International.

Harris, R. Laird. *Theological Wordbook of the Old Testament, Volumes 1 & 2*. Chicago: Moody Bible Institute, 1980.

Hayford, Jack W. *Spirit Filled Life Bible*. Nashville: Thomas Nelson, 1991.

Keller, Werner. *The Bible As History*. New York: William Morrow & Company, 1981.

Magiera, Janet M. *Aramaic Peshitta New Testament Translation*. Truth or Consequences: LWM Publications, 2005.

Pillai, Bishop K. C. *Light through an Eastern Window*. East Stanwood: Inter-Faith Bible Seminar

———. *The Orientalisms of the Bible, Volume 1*. Kingsport: Munkus, 1969.

Prat, Ferdinand. *Jesus Christ His Life, His Teaching, and His Work, Volume 2*. Milwaukee: The Bruce Publishing Co, 1950.

Robinson, Chas S. *Studies of Neglected Texts*. New York: The Century Company, 1883.

Rops, Daniel. *Jesus And His Times, Volume 2*. New York: E.P. Dutton & Company, 1954.

Sayce, A. H. *The Early History of the Hebrews*. 2nd ed. London: Rivingtons, 1899.

Seiss, Joseph A. *The Gospel in the Stars*. 1882. Illust. Ed. Grand Rapids: Kregel, 1982.

Spurgeon, Charles Haddon, updated by Roy H. Clarke. *The Treasury of David*. 1834–1892. Nashville: Thomas Nelson, 1997.

Strong, James. *The New Strong's Exhaustive Concordance of the Bible*. Nashville: Thomas Nelson, 1990.

Wierwille, Victor Paul. *Jesus Christ Our Passover*. New Knoxville: American Christian Press, 1980.

———. *Jesus Christ Our Promised Seed*. New Knoxville: American Christian Press, 1982.

Wight, Fred H. *Manners and Customs of Bible Lands*. Chicago: Moody Bible Institute, 1953.

Wigram, George V., and Ralph D. Winter. *The Word Study Concordance.* Wheaton: Tyndale House, 1978.

Winter, Ralph D., and Roberta H. *The Word Study New Testament.* Wheaton: Tyndale House, 1978.

Youngman, Bernard R. *The Lands and Peoples of the Living Bible.* New York: Bell Publishing Company, 1982.

Printed in the United States
By Bookmasters